Omens From the Flight of Birds
The first 101 days of Jimmy Carter

OMENS FROM THE FLIGHT OF BIRDS

The First 101 Days of Jimmy Carter

A Collective Journal by Writers & Artists

Edited by Stephen Vincent

Momo's Press   1977   San Francisco

Acknowledgement to the
San Francisco Art Commission
and the Capricorn-Asunder Gallery
(Ansel Wettersten, curator)
where the pages were first exhibited.

Special Note: The letters reproduced
herein ("February 4", "February 24",
"March 12", "April 5", and "April
19") are fictions and do not represent
the views of any real person, living
or dead.

ISBN 0-917672-05-4 (paper)
0-917672-06-2 (cloth)

Book Design by Jon Goodchild
Typesetting by Alphabet Express
    of San Francisco.
Printed in the United States of
    America

Momo's Press,
Box 14061, San Francisco
California 94114

for the writers and artists
who made this book possible
and Lucas Andrew McGee-Vincent
born June 7, 1977

Introduction

In November, 1976, not long after the Presidential election, Michael Myers and I were talking about Jimmy Carter's future. Like many others, no doubt, we were curious as to what kind of President he'd make and how our lives might change during his administration. Would Carter impinge on our daily consciousness as Nixon had done, as Ford had tried to do, or would he release the country back into itself? From our vantage , January looked like a fresh starting point for the Republic. Carter would come to Washington with a relatively clear conscience and the possibility of presenting a new vision to the American people.

But how would we react? We decided to ask a number of artists and writers to participate in a collective journal, a daybook. Each participant would take a page or two, five or six times during Carter's first 101 days in office, and create a response, direct or indirect, to the ongoing Administration. The response could take any form the writer/artist chose: poem, story, diary entry, document, cartoon, photograph, collage, drawing, whatever. The idea was to reveal and illuminate the character and spirit of life with/under Carter.

Later, I looked up *inaugurate* in *The American Heritage Dictionary:*

1. To induct into office by a formal ceremony (Latin *inaugurare*, to take omens from the flight of birds, to consecrate, install: *in*, in *augurare*, to augur, from *augur*, soothsayer.)

Wonderful, I had my title: **Omens From the Flight of Birds:** *The First 101 Days of Jimmy Carter*. Contributors would be like birds carrying messages, or soothsayers naming the signs of the new regime. I invited eighteen writers and six artists to participate, people who were in touch with both private and public imaginations. Though we all lived in either the San Francisco Bay area or Northern California, we reflected different geographies, backgrounds and aesthetics. The writing began, calendars in hand, on January 20, Inauguration Day, and completed itself on April 29. What we have, ideally, is a collectively-wrought omen.

STEPHEN VINCENT

Calender of Contents

aretha franklin sings the finale
to the inaugural gala
looking like God just socked her in the jaw
resplendant in her flowing gown
with the humility of a holiness church soloist
a rare almost comical gaze
kind of looks like president carter's
christian scientist fundamentalist gaze
rocking out on God bless america

DAVID HENDERSON

Chronicle
Carter Arrives in Capital

Laughing All the Way

JACK FROST

Computer Ripple (with Andy)

hysteria's most modern racetrack

" . . . the shame of guilt of the pardon"

"We look back in history to see we don't step in
the same manhole as the man in front"

"the sort of place that could be made really elegant"
(teacher of playwriting and part-time traditional
jazz clarinetist) "liquorstick" (Will) Feb 2.

Tom Raworth

To Take Omens From

turned on *as the world turns* thursday but it was some newsy thing pre-empting. swore at the tv set, turned it off. realized a while later that was probably the inauguration. beginning my film today (*pauline & the mysterious pervert*). had final rehearsal last sunday. 2 people showed up. angel & i promised each other to go on a binge at the end of the day, no matter what happened, so it was appropriate. trouble is, we cant drink. it makes him throw up & gives me a neck ache. so we whined around at mary ann's house (where the rehearsal was scheduled), then she & ratch took us under their wings & insisted we down some wine. saw robt duncan this week & he guessed accurately when i asked him to guess how many showed up for final rehearsal. "how'd you know?," i rudely insisted. "my dear," he shrugged, "i was in the theater for *years*! directed stein. ahh! it helps to type-cast, because whatever personal style the actor has they revert to it under stress (such as opening night), & all your suggestions will wilt away." well, i did type cast. not that it's going to be much use if they all drop the hell out.

got a cinematographer, tho; my first choice, in fact. thusly: susie griffin gave a party for adrienne rich & while there, sandy boucher came up to me, asking, "how's the press?" "o, i'm not doing it any more." "why?" "making movies." so half an hour later, ann hershey walks up. "why didnt you tell me you were gonna make a film?" "i did. i asked did you want to do camera." "o. what'd i say?" "you said you were too busy." "well, that's true." she nodded, & walked off. half an hour later she came up again. "who's your crew?" "dont have a crew. they just got divorced." she laughed & walked off. a few minutes later, back again. "what equipment do you have?" "no equipment." she shook her head & walked away. half an hour later, back again. "who's backing you?" "nobody." "where's the money coming from?" "no money." she threw back her head, burst out laughing, & when she was able, said, "& you're starting next week, i suppose." i looked startled, probly, & said, "as a matter of fact, our final rehearsal is next sunday." she hugged me. "you'll do it, too, you crazy lady." then adrienne & i visited for a bit, & alma talked us all into going to the bacchanal for late drinks, & ann came up & put her arm around my shoulders. "i'll give you five days." she said. so we started today—right on schedule!

"The President's lips move too little for the deaf to read them."
—Radio Newscast, January 21

In the morning the American River is full of fishers. From the old bridge I see ducks, gulls and men. Far upriver a gauntlet of fishermen is lined bank to bank across a sandbar. They seem part of the river, stumps or the wreck of a weir. Downriver fishermen gather along a sandbar heaped brown and dry at midstream. The river is low. One of the fishermen walks to the middle of the sandbar, pulls down his waders, squats in the dead grass to shit. His white butt is brilliant in the morning sun.

Barrow's Goldeneye ducks, black and white, the males with black heads and halfmoons on their cheeks, stay in deep pools beside the steep north bank. They bob in the sun, idly preening, then flip swiftly into a dive. They swim fast underwater, as fast as flight. Among the small ducks, the gulls are enormous, ship-like. When two children on the bluff high above the birds heave some rocks which explode into the water, the ducks fly instantly, feathers whistling, in straight lines upstream. The gulls, ponderous and creaky, lift their wings in alarm before taking off and circling to the other side of the river.

I walk down to the bank, dip my hands into the icy water. I slurp a mouthful, and my teeth ache for an instant. Three Canadian geese fly over my head, muttering, climbing to clear the bridge. They fly through the V between the two spans and disappear. Just upstream a young boy is fishing on the bank. Bored or hypnotized from watching his line, he missed the geese. He is shrunken inside a bulky yellow sweatshirt. A large man, perhaps the boy's father, comes along the bank above us. His thick plaid coat is huge enough that he seems whithered inside it too. He has a can of beer in his fist, cradled into the flap of the coat. "Any bites, Jay?" he calls. The boy shakes his head.

Billy Carter is easier to read than the President. Puking on BBC microphones, swiping whiskey from reception tables, he is surely more like people I know than any President's relative in history. Small consolation. He is also the shadow of death behind the born-again President.

TOM SCHMIDT

24

Phone Conversation of the Day

"You sound like Donald Duck."
                    Jimmy Carter (in Washington)
"I *am* Donald Duck."
          Walter Mondale (in Bonn)

                              —from aRb

English is the linguistic by-product of forty years worth of invasions of Britain by three Germanic tribes which began in the year 409. It took them about 150 years to gain control of the entire nation. The earliest English poetry (in Anglian dialect passed on through much later West Saxon scribes) dates from about 650. But it is only with Alfred the Great, king of Wessex, in the ninth century, that written English begins to take off. It is worth noting that in the older manuscripts, the language of the poetry differs greatly from that of the prose (suggesting poetry's roots in the oral tradition, a cool culture product as Levi-Strauss would say), and that it is in the prose that the origins of modern (constantly heating) English are found. Even in the early days, the rate of change seemed fast: "And certaynly our langage now vsed varyeth ferre from that which was vsed and spoken whan I was borne," writes Caxton, 1490. The pen is still new to our fingers, the pre-programmed electronic typewriter (or the manu-script-collating OCCULT computer program, with its language of "slave-text" and "master-text") a hallucination hurtling us into the future.

RON SILLIMAN

Cluster Piece:

imagine   Aeolus
riding   birds
visiting   the
island   nations
in the old way
while in America
the cowboy and
the   baseball
player   are   the
        heroes

it is January in America
the wild birds are pecking their way free of the ice

Honor
Future
Feather
Champion

"We had a whole bunch of hens," said John, "that wouldn't lay,
and I knew which ones they were, so I went in one morning and I
said, Mamas, you'd better get to laying or I'm going to make stew
out of you. You know who I'm talking to and so do I. I told them
I'd give them one more week, and I did, I gave them a week and
they still didn't lay so I grabbed myself one a day until we'd made
stew out of every last one. I'll get myself some young ones when it
warms up in the spring."

sat easily across the room bent over
the book and whether it is a bird
taken from a tree or time to be home
the ceramic cow or whether it is the live one
out in the field
his is the cluster to be history
as is ours
bent easily and whether it is a cup
or a poem drawn with crayons
some reason
and the air is cut and restored
something that is done every hour
as if the birds had slept

LYN HEJINIAN

Woke up from a strange dream about finding a pill in my skin. Thought I would be hungover as Pat Nolan & Steve LaVoie were here last night. I laid in bed bracing myself until I realized I wasn't. Thank you Jesus. Morning routine: start water for tea, bicycle for Chronicle, back in time for water boiling. 2 boiled eggs on English muffin, no coffee, too expensive. Just before leaving for Mrs. Merck's, I change shirts & find a cache of illegal drugs in my pocket. I must have been *really* ripped last Friday to forget them. Mrs. Merck: trimmed two plum trees, a Bartlett pear in very bad shape due to clumsy Merck trimming, & decapitated a bottle brush bush. Take larger limbs home & chainsaw for firewood. To dump, where the lady charges me 2 dollars for the load. She's reading Maya Angelou. Drop Lani at unemployment office & then up to pick up Kirk's junk from remodeling. A white official car pulled up outside the house. I thought "Oh-oh." It was the building inspector & he hit on Flip, the carpenter, for his roofing permit which of course Flip did not have. *"And that's called getting caught,"* Flip yells down from the roof after the guy left, *"She-it."* The dump lady's reading some newspaper & later I wonder if it was Muhammad Speaks because when I joked with her to leave enough money from the $5 for some ribs, she said, "I don't eat ribs." In all our many conversations I don't remember her letting on she was Muslim. Stopped off at Wine & The People for money from Kirk. "I got $15,000 from the bank last week," Kirk says, "and I've got $5,000 left. I'm going to kill that guy who sold me that house. Dry rot. And *then* the permit man shows up. Was he a bald guy, etc.." "Yeah." "Too bad I wasn't there," Kirk says, "We might have been able to work something out." He tells me a story about bribery in the Army. Home. Persephone & I bicycle to the nursery for red onions & lettuce sets. We plant them in back. I worry about my irrigation system working, the drought, etc. Dinner & Warrior BBall on TV. I'm tired. I come into my room & wonder what to do. I take the dope I forgot in my pocket. Read all about Charles Olson on Mescaline. I wonder if certain people like Charles Olson because he proved you could be obviously bonkers & still be an academic. I notice Steve's calendar & realize it's my day. After writing everything up, I go check the new lettuce for snails & piss in the backyard to ease the drought situation. Every little bit helps.

KEITH ABBOTT

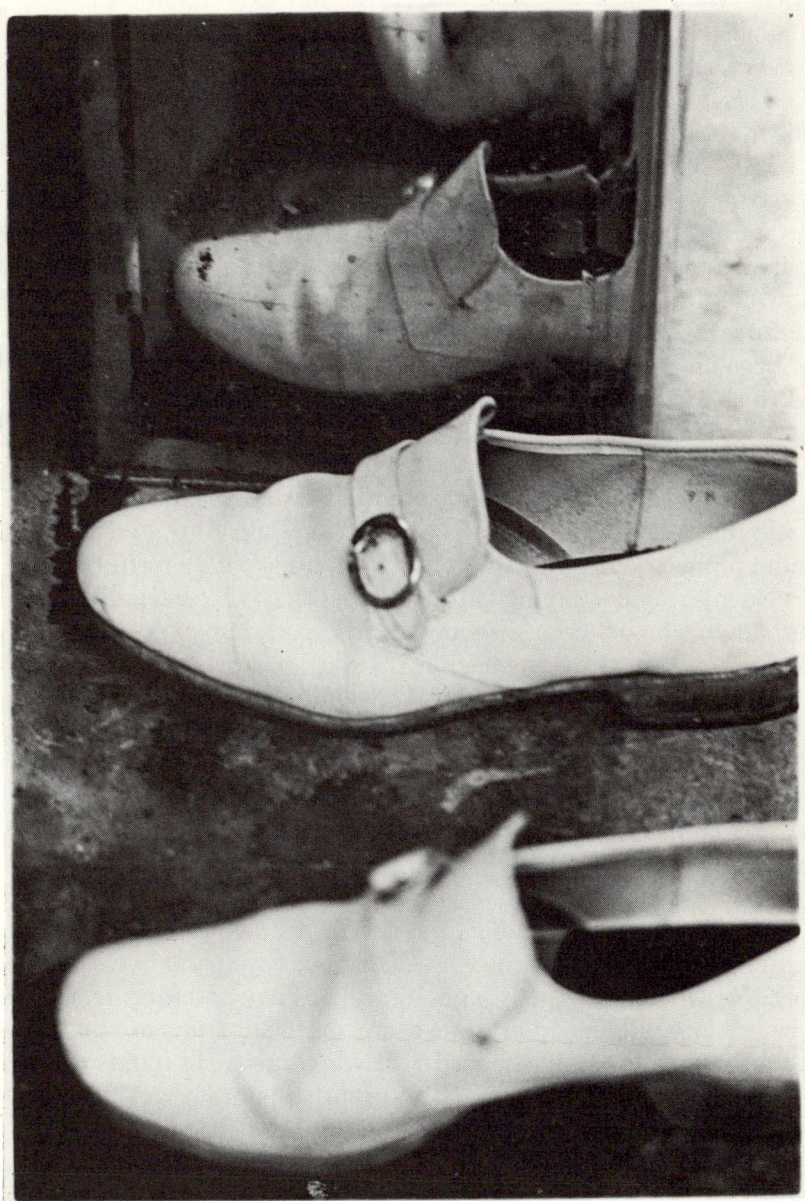

Robert Rusk

27

In the morning there. Carter slipping on ice. A photograph in the Chronicle. His arms up. His smile off. As if sliding into second. Actually The White House driveway. A military attache behind him. Article says the attaches brief case is "full of top secret nuclear codes". Over the photograph, in dark bold letters, the caption says, "Carter Dances On Ice".

This is the week of "Roots". Every night on the t.v. A dark rippling in the air. Are we into a re-run of the sixties?

Three inches below Jimmy's dancing (slipping, sliding) feet is "odd couple" captioned photograph of Eldrige Cleaver and Charles Colson, born again, loving brother Christians. Eldridge's face looks bloated, sunk. Colson works to look like "the thinker", a Rodin hand up to his chin. Article says Cleaver's "conversion began in the south of France in 1975 when he was feeling low. He was watching the sky and began to see faces in the moon, faces of his old heroes—Fidel Castro and Mao Tse-tung. Then, when the face turned to Jesus, he began to cry uncontrollably." Is that why his eyes look swollen?

Is it too much to imagine Carter slipping down the page to join Colson and Cleaver in Baptismal embrace? All born again?

In the evening I give a poetry reading in Palo Alto. I wear a real peanut pinned on my vest. People ask why. I say it's a fertility pin. It's also my way of keeping in touch with Carter. It's telepathic sympathetic magic. One false move and I crush him or eat him. People get jittery at the suggestion.

It is my theory of the peanut. When the President was still down in Plains, before coming to take over in Washington, he would give his news conferences outside the warehouse on his peanut farm. Wasn't it symbolic? Instead of standing in front of his house, or out on a golf course, to stand in front of a barn full of peanuts. Visions of peanut butter, oil and salivating American mouths. That warehouse his own sense of source and power.

Or was he just packaging himself? Each statement a little plastic or aluminum bag of mild roast. A suspicious country. I bet, however, especially when things get rough, he will be back and forth from Washington to Plains. Everytime he begins to slip, or is not quite sure what to do, he will be back in the warehouse. His hands will run through the peanuts, hold, crack and eat them until he gets his power back. It will either succeed miraculously or bore us to death.

Tonight, before driving down to the reading, when I held Debra, I got a kick, an actual large kick in my stomach. The kid we are going to have in June is actually there!

STEPHEN VINCENT

Tight Rope

THE HIGH WIRE IS JUST RIGHT FOR CYCLING   DOING A
HANDSTAND ON THE HANDLEBARS & A SLOW SOMERSAULT
ON THE WAY DOWN

      there was a family of trapeze artists once (the flying flamingos)
      they were shot down in the middle of their act by some crazed
      off-duty bocce ball players
      blood rained on the crowd
      they learned not to peek at tragedy
      the populace loves losers more than love sometimes

THE TIGHT WIRE IS FOR CRUISING WITH NO HANDS
DOING A WHEELIE WHILE EATING A BAG OF PEANUTS
GROOVE ON THE APPLAUSE FROM BELOW   THEN CARE-
FULLY CLIMB DOWN WITHOUT SPILLING YOUR SMILE

ALEJANDRO MURQUIA

There Is An Incessant Party Goin' On Downstairs, But Do Presidents Ever Know About Such Things . . .

The only interesting thing about Jimmy Carter's pre-inauguration celebration was that it included Freddie Prinze. The celebration occurred one week ago and broadcast live on television, with Freddie Prinze wearing his new and skinny personality like an omen of things to come.

I wonder if the Carter family was embarrassed by having Freddie on their guest list. The young comedian, with his self-effacing string of Puerto-Rican-Hungarian jokes, made a career of his ethnocentric neuroses. He provided escapist entertainment for a country that rewarded him by inviting him to a party.

I like a good party. A good party doesn't mean standing around sipping cocktails and bein' official. I wonder if that's what they do in government. I don't doubt it. And I don't think Jimmy Carter's any different than anyone else in the White House, even though he wears jeans and has the flair to appoint Andrew Young as U.N. ambassador. All rednecks wear jeans. It doesn't mean shit. And if he were really different, he wouldn't be president, cuz different and president don't go together. And as far as Andrew Young goes, well—with his big mouth he may not last too long as ambassador to anything anyway. Or he may pull a fast one and be more malleable than we think. I don't know. But what I know about is parties—and Jimmy Carter probably doesn't know too much about giving a real good one, like those hot and heavy soirees Arnim usedta throw over there at that flat he usedta rent on Laguna street . . . O my god, talk about sluts and saints! It was better than any Labelle concert.

They say people like to party during a depression. That's when all the lavish Busby Berkeley productions started happening, and Hollywood blossomed. People, they say, like to sing and dance when they're poor. They like to sing their blues away, that's what they say. They'll spend their last dollar on movies like "Jaws", "The Exorcist", "The Omen", "It's Alive", "Demon Seed", "Black Sunday"; "The Exorcist Part Two" "The Devil In The Closet" "Hangin' Out Wid The Devil" "Coming Out Wid The Devil"; that's what's known as escapist entertainment.

I don't know about all that, but I do know one thing. There is an incessant party goin' on downstairs, and it's keeping me awake. The music never stops, and I don't know where it's coming from or who's dancing. It's not the second floor, and it's certainly not the first floor—they're too busy worrying about survival. It's not us. We don't believe in parties starting at eight o'clock in the morning.

And another thing. Yesterday Freddie Prinze decided he was "tired of it all." Hollywood had descended on his halfbreed ass like some sort of pink-faced angel chewing on a Cuban cigar. He danced the minstrel shuffle just long enough to blow his head off. He was what you would call a star.

JESSICA HAGEDORN

After the day in Diane Di Prima's Gertrude Stein workshop and
the week of *Roots*—I think of Adrienne Rich's discussion of encoding in
women's work—the hidden female/feminist meanings that must be decoded
by us, now that we have a context and are aware that these meanings are
there, hidden.

    Stein: . . . she is feeling that the grasses grow four times yearly and does
        she furnish a house as well . . . let her think of a stable man and a
        stable can be a place where they care for Italians every day . . .
My own poem: . . . *or do I cry for myself / fifty-four, white / stabled. . .*
stable, stabled, enslaved. Denial of the mother, of the female, denial of
nature. And denial is impossible. Then rape, murder, slavery, ecological
disasters.

    Stein: *did she see someone as she was advancing and did she remove
what she had and did she lose what she touched. . .* masculine flight from
touch—leading to rape, murder, slavery.

    Roots—what was there for women in Kunta's African village, his para-
dise of freedom? Only Identification, that seductive snare. How would the
story have been told by a woman: rejected by sons, denied contact with the
gods, despised? Kunta's beloved Fanta became an American quickly; being
Massa's concubine was no great change . . . and then Kizzie, to her black
lover—*I won't fetch for you, I'm enough of a slave in my life: I won't be a
slave for you.*

    Stein connects masculine rationalism with enslavement . . . *let her think
of a stable man and wandering and repetition of counting. Count to ten. He
did. He did not.* Dualism, rationalism, stability, exploitation. Tom Moore's
angry wife, futile on her pedestal. And he says fucking girls on slave row is
one of the joys of civilized life.

    Count to ten. He did. He did not. A day's immersion in Stein's circular
time—dualism grows meaningless—I feel released into my life—ambivalent
and circular—*the grasses grow four times yearly.*

FRANCES JAFFER

The Invention of the White Race

English came to Jamestown. Now early on in the 17th Century they thought: *Hey, let's find a nice river, settle down, make those Indians slaves and lay back like the Spaniards down South.* This didn't work. Indians just fled back to their farms & hamlets to watch, on guard. This meant English had to work themselves, plant strange corn and all. Consequently, they starved.

This is what you call a labor problem. The rich Dukes and Lords couldn't handle a "new world" unless it could turn a dollar. Since those Indians won't be slaves, they brought in small farmers whose lands they stole, debtors, crooks, scum, and workers half-dead from big slums in England & made *them* slaves. They said: "At least in the New World you don't got wars and you can get religion any way you want and life is slick so just work 30 years and you'll be 'free' to stake out your *own* land (maybe), and all you gotta do is kill a Indian." Meanwhile they brought over Africans. These lords didn't like the Africans, but they didn't like their own poor folks much either. They didn't care: They had a labor problem; they needed slaves.

These poor white folks came to Jamestown convinced life was gonna be a breeze compared to hell-hole England. Rich lords were making giant plantations for tobacco, a great money-maker even then. But the new plantations suffered from economic breakdown after breakdown. They had depressions even back in 1660. Meanwhile the big planters were arguing with each other on how to steal land from the Indians. Even then they knew the way out was to spread out. The rich bastards started fighting with each other on what's the best way to kill Indians & who'd make the most money off of doing it. Meanwhile, the poor folks couldn't stand it no more. In 1676 they rose up in arms—Africans and English both—led by a guy named Bacon. Black and white fought side by side. They called it Bacon's Rebellion. The rich bastards were taken by surprise because what had been just a quarrel between themselves got turned against them *all*. The rebels sacked Jamestown, threw out the Company that owned all the shit, and set up poor folks rule. Governor Berkeley scurried into exile across Chesapeake Bay and schemed. As history might have it, the rebels got sold out and lost.

Governors and all the rich Lords thought: *"This can't happen again. We both got big monies in this operation. Profits just got invented and we gonna make it work!"* After a while, they come up with a perfect idea: **Let's make slaves Black!**

They look at the English. Well, the new Big Monies got their way in England cause Cromwell did his revolution to beat back the old-fashioned lords who wanted feudalism with just plain serfs. But to do this Cromwell told the serfs: "Fight with me and you'll be free!" Of course this was a little exaggeration, this freedom, but now that they weren't serfs it'd be hard for the Big Monies to make them slaves *for life!* Nope. That's *too much.* Besides, who gonna be police? Virginia is too far away to always have a army & it aint a island like Jamaica where off-shore boats can always come to the rescue.

Then they look at the Africans. Hmmm. Let's make *them* slaves—for life! A flunky goes up to Duke Big Wad and says: "See, Boss, it's like this. We make the English be indentured servants for 7 years, even less than now, and we make the Africans indentured servants for *life.* We'll make the time less and less for the white trash and we'll make it more and more for them Black trash. We can make laws what say no more inter-marriage which has gotten outta hand anyway—disgusting criminal intimacy specially since neither Black nor white care to stop—and we'll give rewards to the white trash for capturing runaway Black trash. Don't you see, Boss? We can tell who the slaves are cause they *look* different, they're Black. Right now both the white trash and the Black trash like each other cause they all hate us. We gotta get the white trash happy to work for us so's to keep the Black trash down and then they don't both kick our ass. Soon all we need to say is: 'See, at least *you* aint a nigger, so shut up!' what you think, Boss?"

Boss gave the nod.

Thus the poor white was made to join the Slave Patrols and made to fold to his bosom the snake that stings him.

This then was the invention of the white race.

HILTON OBENZINGER

You May Kill The Dreamer
But Never The Dream.

You May Kill An Honest Soul
But Never Honestly.

You May Kill A Warrior
And Never Know Peace

RENE YANES   PHOTO BY WILFRED CASTANO

In the shadows
during the hours when the big
cats get rewarded and
vampires feast on innocent
necks
I see the yellow light in the far
room
where my mother sits stitching on a knitted dress
for some deluded
starlet
one sequin bead upon another
like days upon a lifetime for her
children
I see the dim light
the dress on my mother's knees
as she is bent
like a rocking chair
and I am angry and
ashamed
my mother doesn't
wear the dresses with the glitter
and she catches me looking and smiles
and I wonder where
the anger is coming from and
who it is for
and I smile back full of love for her
while unable to contain myself, I yell at her
to stop working so late
on some dress that
will never be worn on her back
and she puts it against me
and I hate the dress and what it represents
she assures me it won't take long to finish
and the light now is in her eyes
and I go to my bed and
wait for the sun
which will rise
3 decades since
that time
and my understanding of where my anger
is from and who it is for
becomes redefined—there are
2 classes. Those
who work to survive and
those who live for profit
The hour of vampires and big cats
is waning
and many others awake in the
same light that took me 3 decades to see
that very same light that broke in my mother's eyes.

JOSELYN IGNACIO

For The Full Snow Moon

There was a woman whose husband died before she gave birth to their child.

When the child was born at last, it was that time of the year when the snow is drifted thickly against the camp and when animals burrow in the dark and people wrap themselves and huddle over their fires.

It was quiet for a long time. And then one day the ice began to crack in the stream and the snow began running away as water.

The mother packed the baby on her back and walked out towards the stream. She was alone there when she met a man in the shape of her dead husband. The man spoke nothing to her but at the sight of him she was so overcome with grief and longing that she could think of nothing but to follow him. Leaving the baby beside the stream, she ran after him and was just in time to see him disappear inside the entrance to a narrow cave. In despair she realized her human flesh would never pass through the small gap in those rocks and, as she wept, she suddenly felt her body shrivel and turn cold. Her tears dried on her skin and her voice was stopped and her long tongue played on the cold silent air. She dragged her length across the snow towards the cave and crawled between the rocks, and so left this world for the darkness below.

When two women came to the stream later in the day, they discovered the baby nearly frozen. They searched everywhere for the mother but found only her tracks in the snow and, after following them a certain distance, they saw nothing except what appeared, to their amazement, to be the wavering track of a snake in the snow.

BEVERLY DAHLEN

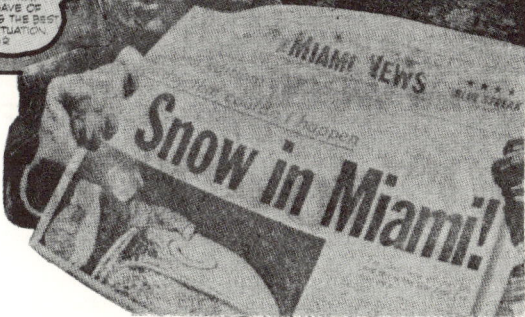

JACK FROST

Plains, Georgia
February 4, 1977

Hello My Pal,

Well wouldn't you know it, ole Ma Nature picks the start-out of Jimmy's administration to shut down the juice and transform the currency, they got snow over everything, and hell, it's like Miz Lillian says, Jimmy might as well of gotten hisself elected Emperor of the Ukraine or some damn *Baltic* province if it's going to be this energy snickerty-snack all the time. Now they saying the microwaves are eating on the insides of our heads with this radiation nonsense, and maybe Mr. Coffee, too, but I figure Jimmy to fix it, he knows nukes. He send the Buffalo folks crockpots, appropriate 'em right from Treasury. Poor Chip, he had to go on north for a look-see and he don't know snow from cocaine. And out west they got just the opposite going, rocks where the rivers was a catfish belly-up all over, little anked chirren begging for a drink of water, and that pissant Jerry Brown can't do a thing about it. Whole damn state of California can meditate at once and it won't drip a drop. Some ole boy down the station trying to tell me the other day we caused this trouble by shooting deodorant into the air. Destroyed the O Zone. The hell, I said, then we still got the P Zone and on down before we get in any *real* trouble!

But pal, the truth is, it's bringing me down, the people, the noise, the lights that pop, all this fizzling for nothing. One more tourist lady snap a Kodiak in my face I'm like to launch a dead Pabst tin at her. I been drinking too much. I been waking in the night to the white in the black and I go to the window and there's nothing out there. It's like the snow is all in me. I listen for the breathing in the house and comes back at me the chuff of my own dying lungs. Some days I stay home from the peanut office, stay home here warm listen to Dolly Parton and she sounds like melting snow, running water, and her wigs is pure heaven. Brother, you know I like to win, and I do believe in Jimmy, but the chill been in my bones too often now. Can't eat on hope forever.

Your good buddy,

Billy Carter

After long sleeplessness, money worries, dreamed a mandala of moons, Buffalo (our dog who died in the desert) there, tail thumping, tongue & wet nose & fur when I hug him, Jimmy Carter by the grassy door, fossil seashells, transformations, playing soccer with a black dude who holds; drop everything! W.C. Fields is coming! out by his blue pick-up Jan's father, who died in 1953, plays a bottleneck blues
"dontcha leave my baby
dontcha put me on"
Kids gone for their week in Oakland. Furiously cleaned the stove for two hours. Jan left for walk, I drank Morning Thunder tea & smoked a little Ridge Primo, worked awhile on my space narrative, SEEDSTONE:

Anywhere, except in the inner space of journey-time you count out your life & breath by the way the planets & suns hum round you. 1 Zain year equals 1.2 Narayan years equals 1.4 where I sit on Seed-stone under a diffused noon of pearlgray cloud remembering. I could coliate the calendars for you. It doesn't matter. Anywhere you are time either opens its mouth like grayedged ocean or space to where photons turn dark or suddenly a known date comes rushing & the numbers rumble ahead of my face like a fall of water . . .

Made phonecalls, Poetry In The Schools business. Dug holes in garden strip by street, old Asian man "ah! you are planting trees!" I nod. Business of the Folsom Workshop being shut down, Warden Thomas writes "assure you that the action taken by this institution was appropriate at this point in time," meanwhile Mike Wojczuk says Jerry & Pancho are both in the hole on weird synchronus charges. Played frisbee with the gray wind awhile. Tea: coast old-man sagebrush, yerba santa, peppermint & savory. Got a close look at the big feral mexican yellowhead parrots, gnashing pyracantha berries, make them high, stripes of aztec scarlet on the wing. Jan home bushed & cramping, I jogged up to track & ran a mile in 6:01.6, hot shallow drought bath, made dinner, eggplant-vegie-sherry-lemon-cheese stirfry & rice, "I'm a lucky woman to have you cook for me," yum, quiet, dark, time, bewildered. Hard to believe the school burned down.
"dontcha know I love you
dontcha close the door"

John Oliver Simon

Manong Gallo*

had a vision when he was only ten years old.
Told his great grandmother what he saw.
She thought her grandson was a little crazy.

> "The woman in the sky
> said I was the son of the forest.
> Take care of the trees, rocks, animals,
> insects, grass, rivers, mountains.
> They belong to you; they are your family."

When Manong Gallo was eighteen years old,
he climbed the tallest coconut tree to the moon.
When he looked down, he saw the great pacific ocean.
He said, "Dagat (ocean) you think you big and wide?
> But you wait! Someday I am going to cross you.
> And I will see the other side of your face."

*Manong: term of endearment for elder Pilipino

AL ROBLES

bird flight

i bet i have never had one day in my life when i havent done one major fuck up. all these books about life after death: seeing the great light at the end of the tunnel; they all talk about seeing their own life spread out before them, & the agony they felt at all the wrong things they had done. jesus, i could spend my whole life bent over in shame. cant wait to get to purgatory, where i can relive it all in GLORIOUS COLOR!

the latest major flaw in my character has resulted in not being able to rescue alice paul (the author of the equal rights amendment) out of the rest home her nephew slammed her in. i could have driven up to the door, put her in the car, driven her back to her house, & kicked out her nephew, & gotten her a nurse, but i chickened out. i could have hired a lawyer to petition that she get awarded control of her own life. but i didnt know how, or who to turn to. i asked around a lot. made a lot of calls; did what it felt like i was able to do, all the way from california, when she's locked up in new jersey. but the lawyer we had counted on (katherine rora-back) has not called back for 3 weeks. alice's property goes up for sale tomorrow. her house. the place she wants to go home to. on account of me not knowing my head from my butt, she has no chance (according to the 3 lawyers i talked to today in new haven, bridgeport & ridgefield) to save her home. whose fault is that? i can blame roraback for not returning my calls; i can blame her nephew for locking her up; i can blame the women who have been her friends for years; i can blame my husband for taking up my time in arguments; but i know damn well, if i hadnt botched it, she would stand a chance. & because i botched it, alice will not have the ownership of her own home. the most i have gotten is a verbal promise from the renters who want to buy that they will fix up the place & welcome her to live there. at $350 a month. good, alta. you did real good. if i drank, i would cer-tainly spend the evening in an appropriate stupor. instead, i guess i'll go walk by the ocean & hope i can feel something for myself besides hate; & something for the world besides despair. as alice wrote to the woman helping her fight for women's suffrage in nevada, "i am in despair." jesus, i wish i could have done it right. then you'd have your home to go to, lady. i dont have to ask you to forgive me. you dont even know i was trying. i just have to look at this world every day, & see that i am no better now than i was as a child, when i vowed that by this time i would have the strength of a saint, & so be able to perform miracles.

Poem

1
The object-nature of the ocean
the oceanic joke
the great colorlessness
of the ocean
washing away the nearest streets,
and today the president's first
news conference.
I was a sucker for democrats
in my youth.

2
He will be glad who
remembers her visit
and utterly cancels
any aspect of dreaming it
by fucking with her.

3
I was a tireless voter
even Humphrey got my nod.
Now it's the presidency of the personal life
with round heads smiling
over NBC & ABC ads
makes me think
if you liked the "captive nations"
you will love "human rights".

Tom Mandel

MICHAEL MYERS

"When things are hard to get everyone wants one"

"bands of music" (arthur bryant)

the pick of centuries
of what still defines
'valuable': own the land

affects not the balance but the tone

'one evening saul was sitting beside his fire
in the village of ogham'

matthew boulton
"you'll be able to avoid
anything you've ever dreamed of"

QUIN

becoming good

'she can't live up to being bionic—she'll
burn herself out'   nod.

the short life of electricity (he wrote)

reality is a mirror
        dear diary

a football co-operative called 'our team'

salmon cat food

TOM RAWORTH

Cluster Piece

the second thing was a beginning
you may use this
                    But I live in retrospect, which is different
from living in the past. I seem only to feel an experience
after it is over, as I think of it. Events return to me as
stories in their fullest force. During my initial encounter
with an experience everything seems unreal, and the experience
becomes real only later. History is a retrospect in a
similar way, and hence today is an enduring tale.
                                        You were
given that name because it summoned the force of the hero
whose name it was before you.
                            You asked if I had improvised
much of my work. Writing by its very nature prevents
improvisation, in fixing the words on a page. Do you mean to
ask if I write spontaneously and never rewrite and revise?
The answer is no. That is, I do write spontaneously sometimes,
tired or drinking wine and without forethought or plan, but
that only provides a few things to work with later. I revise
and revise. Or do you mean to ask if I talk out my ideas and
images, improvising in that way? Sometimes. I like to tell
stories and relate anecdotes. Even more, I like to hear them.
The older I get the more I prefer other people's talk to my
own. That is about as accurate a history as you're going to
get.
     In time magic wears out as all magics must. The divinity
of rulers is such a magic, and so is the infallibility of
justice.
              There is an exercise for poets that helps to call
attention to the difference between strong and weak words.
You write one word on each of many slips of paper—the number
is not important—say twenty. You turn the words face down
and randomly pick the paper slips up one at a time, writing
down each word in order. You allow yourself "the," "a" or "an,"
"and," and "is." That is your poem. The weaker words are
immediately apparent. "Magnificent," for example, says
nothing. "Potato" and "crush" are clear.

LYN HEJINIAN

on the eve of the birthday of the great emancipator
here is the southern man who in history was disenfranchised
by Honest Abe more than a hundred years ago
now as president of the nation Lincoln built.
he is a strange man who speaks
in the voice of a tenor in a choir
who is poised to almost genuflect
before a nation
a simple way of faith.
he is the one
scientist and farmer
holy man and father
president and human
from back in the woods of the southern land
who is more careful than the Pope
in gesture and garment.
does this man know of the violence against Blacks
that marked Georgia's history?
Has his Christian countenance ever seen a lynching?
Has he ever seen a chain-gang peopled by Black men,
women and children of Georgia, their legs ripped raw
by the reign of iron?
One wonders just what the peaceful countenance
of the christian scientist president has seen
besides the glory.

Dᴀᴠɪᴅ Hᴇɴᴅᴇʀsᴏɴ

I pledge allegiance ..... Jack Loo 1977

JACK LOO

manong osas

sometimes your heart
breaks down

like a bomb

exploding
inside your brain

shattering

back the years
into broken pieces
of glass

inside a child's foot

not knowing
where you've been

like a sharp knife

cutting
the memory
in half

manong osas

give me
your hands
even if
you are crying inside

there is no use
to kill yourself now

when you don't even know
who you are

AL ROBLES

Journey Down Rivers of My Mind

Sunday what a day
Alligators in the bathtub
Timbalero in the hallway
Flamingo on the wall
Paints me stories of
Carribean rides
Thru crazy jungle towns
Where night life meets
In smokey cafes
To snort ice
While dancers
Step thru shadows
Darkly in the light
Drums beat
Awaking of the primal cry—

Flashes on a tramp steamer
cutting a slow turn
before the open land/
tropical and unknown

ALEJANDRO MURQUIA

El Santero Reads A Poem About
Human Survival In Chile On President's
26th Day In Office While A Daggert Floats By.

RENE YANES   PHOTO BY WILFRED CASTANO

A Valentine

for LZ—as far
as the eye can see
the ear hears
song clear as the sun
here on the sea
shore where we
feel free

from **The Redbooks**

What is to be done but nothing, and nothing resolutely? Nothing repels so
as the knowledge of limits. The job you could have if you want it, if only,
and what that entails. How one learns to resent the bridge. In the middle of
winter, events of mock-spring. The coffee, dripping, will fill the cup, one's
second. Stained oilcloth covers the beautiful table. Windchimes on the back
porch tinkle and clatter. Cats sleep in the shade. The rule is the better the
weather the later the mail, thus mixed feelings, tho one is so far behind in
one's correspondence any letter is unlikely. Why not say I, says she. Why
choose white shoes, say I. What exactly is one doing, if anything? Deter-
mined to fill these notebooks as if to some purpose, perhaps. One squints,
or scowls. My script or scrawl changes daily, amazed that I can still read it.
Can you?

RON SILLIMAN

i dreamt k____ came back to town. didn't believe it possible; he'd left the
Gazette for a fantastic job on the Sun Times after his series on jails was
picked up nationally. even tho he was gone, i still held on to what we had
had; in my dark moments it comforted me; i knew love like that was possible, & for awhile, we got to have it. but since he had dropped out of my life
life, i'd decided it must have been one-sided. last spring, a man at the cafe
was telling about a friend of his who had had "a searing love affair" & how
he was torn; to go with it, or opt for the wife. he chose his marriage. i of
course thot of me & k____ & told the man about my affair with him; how it
takes so much courage for two people to allow themselves to feel that
deeply, & that the two of us had equal courage. the guy said, "you dont
mean k____!" & i said, "yeah. how'd you know?" he was silent a bit, then;
"there is a name he speaks—not often, cause he doesnt talk much, but every
time he says her name, he sounds like a man. i want to feel that sometime in
my life." this stranger then looked at me & said, "is your name alta?"

   so it was not one-sided. & now k____s back in town. we met acciden-
tally; met again for lunch; days later i was coming out of the bank & saw
him coming out of a whore house. i couldnt speak. of all the men who know
joy, this is the guy. yet he deliberately chose to oppress some woman he
doesnt know, & didnt even ask to be with me! i broke. went home, took an
overdose. my little girl called & saved my life; i vomited, but was too weak
to clean up. angel came home, cleaned me off, made coffee, found the bottle,
called the hospital, & kept me awake & talking. "what happened, buns?"
"they're bigger than i am." "they're bigger?" "yep. there never has been a
man who loved me enuf to give up mistreating women."

   so back to taking refuge in work, & politics. yesterday i met odette at
the cafe & she said, "there's an excellent expose of prostitution in the
Gazette," "the Gazette! who wrote it?" she handed me the paper. "everyone
involved in the street walker scene is a victim . . . the hookers themselves are
probably the primary victims . . ." she said, "let's see—the reporter's name is
k____. is he a friend of yours?"

The Last Chair in Baja

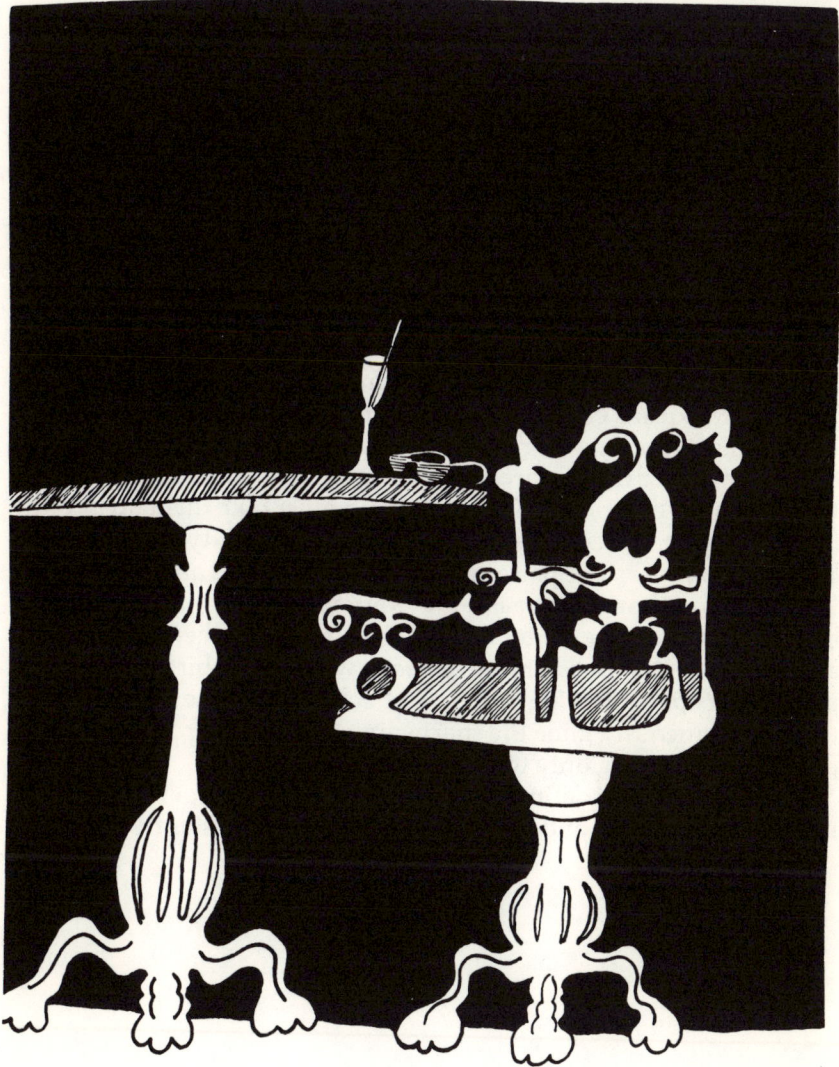

DEBRA MCGEE

Cabo St. Lucas, Baja

At the Hotel Solar. The last large beach on the Pacific side of Baja. Debra and I sit out on the terrace drinking Cuba Libres, orange juice and beer. Watching the sun go down. Behind us the rocky white brown cliffs, the final low mountainous ridge to reach down into the Pacific. In front of us beige sands separate us by maybe a hundred yards from the deep drop off, where the waves turbulently hit, making swimming impossible.

As the sun drops down the horizon to the north, the sky turns orange, then light lavendar, then gray. The wind slows from what was a steady, light afternoon pace. Turning to the south, high over the final low peak of the ridge, birds circle. They are, I later learn, what the Mexicans call "Tijeratas", "scissor tails". English speaking Americans, for whatever reason, call them "frigate", "man of war" or "soaring" birds. They are slender, large, and, except for a severe white breast, solid black. The setting sun must take them up into the formation that we see, floating in circles, at least sixty or seventy birds, if not more. The pattern of their movement is amazing to watch. It is as though there is a gravitational center that pulls each bird in from the large, outer edge of the circle, and then turns it out again, a perfectly orchestrated dance in which each bird flawlessly performs its part, moving gracefully back through the pairs of birds that simultaneously glide the sharpening circles toward the center point, once arriving only to swing back out again.

What causes or defines the center I do not know. When the sun is completely down, and the first star is out, they instantly disappear.

STEPHEN VINCENT

The First Intercollegiate Dance Meet

February 17. I'd forgotten how a gym fills up with the smack of the basketball on the light-splashed floor, the clean sweat smell, the noisy cheering sections. Tonight CSU Sacramento must beat Chico in order to tie for the women's league lead. I like the way Sue Wheeler, Sac State, plays. Slender and golden, she is the darting flame of the team's spirit, blocking shots or stealing the ball each time the game needs turning around.

At the half the Dance Team marches in wearing yellow-striped Hornet socks, green shorts and black leotards, carrying Adidas shoulder bags—a perfect parody of Olympic formality. As half-time announcer, I interview Pam Walker, CSUS athletic information officer.

Pam: That's right, Tom, this is the first Intercollegiate Dance Team. We felt a need for a space for free movement, so we invented it. It gets rid of the unnecessary restrictions of older dance forms.

Tom: But what about *necessary* restrictions, rules of the game.

Pam: Each Intercollegiate Dance Meet creates its own rules to fit the particular time and space.

Tom: And this action going on right now, how is it measured? By time or speed? By form?

Pam: That's simple. It's measured by how good the dancers feel.

When the 20 dancers work in lanes down the court, stringing ribbons of energy across the room, the crowd murmurs approval. Tom Nardinelli, in a referee's costume, moves everywhere backwards, and when he screams penalties the crowd roars with laughter while the dancers ignore him absolutely.

Mary Musler, small and poised, follows the focus of her eyes with pure concentration. Heidi Goodridge suddenly appears at center stage, looking as if she swallowed a ballerina. Karen Schmidt is big, full of strength which, by the look of her face, is a surprise to her. Here she is coach, too, keeping this dance, which she designed, in order.

The horn sounds for the finale. "It's a rugby scrum!" someone says. They stomp their feet like a nest of hornets, and the scrum explodes into a brief moment of football, vicious blocks and tackles in slow motion. When the basketball teams come back to warm up, the court is littered with bodies. The crowd loves it.

TOM SCHMIDT

Read today to the Browning Society. A fine experience. The women loved it. Some of them wept. (Some slept, too!) G.S. was wiped out—she talked of "metamorphosis" etc. Mark, too, was excited and impressed newly by my poems and my reading. He read very well, too—and I begin to see more and more the beauty of his poems. I feel an inferiority of my own poems when I listen—not perhaps very good for me. I wish I understood what it is he means when he gets excited about my poems. I don't really know what it is. Oh well, probably just as well I don't know.

Long talk with S. today—focussing on the "quality of life" question. Problem an odd one, although I fear common—as the quality of life improves, the fear of losing it (dying) gets greater, thus impairing the quality of life! A circle, but not the best kind.

She says something about the need to be more adventurous, and I know she's right. I'll have to really zero in on that one. I know my dream this morning was about being more adventurous—three staircases and I chose the safest but had a sort of yearning for the slippery adventurous one which wasn't really dangerous but was exciting and involved some unpleasantness. It would indeed be nice at my age to become more adventurous. I can see suddenly that that would be the greatest meaning to my next twenty-thirty years—after a life of certain kinds of timidity to go beyond—physically and spiritually . . . .

I suppose becoming a poet and critic and outspoken feminist has been a first step to adventurousness. Perhaps the decision to "go to Greece no matter what" has the beginnings of a more adventurous spirit: not so safe, but more joyous. Oh how I see us in a white Greek house, typing, and then sitting in a Taverna drinking retsina. I think a lifetime of timidity is tiresome—I have *seemed* adventurous (thinking about the people in Hartford, for example), but I have a greater need for adventure. Am I being foolish to think that my spirit is potentially larger than theirs and therefore to limit myself to security even as much as I have done, may be more dangerous for me? (Hubris?) I am beginning to think I am really a poet. I think this means the possibility of a larger risk life, with greater rewards—perhaps I will let myself think this blasphemous thought for a while and see where it gets me . . . .

FRANCES JAFFER

ROBERT RUSK

Snowflakes in Hawaii

I woke up seeing snowflakes and forgot where I was. For an instant I had the distinct impression that snowflakes had descended on Hawaii. Unfortunately, it finally dawned on me that I was in the Midwest, and in a few hours, I had a performance scheduled with Roscoe Mitchell at the Indianapolis Museum of Modern Art. Indianapolis. The very word struck terror in my heart. Like I was King Kong waking to Manhattan in 1931. Like I was Ming the Merciless swishing down Folsom Street to Chaka Khan's "Everlasting Love." Like I was Godzilla trudging through Tokyo in 1967, searching out whatever reptiles might be lurking in the Mitsubishi Department Store, suffering from sheer loneliness . . .

Today I had no interest in Jimmy Carter's lipless smile, or that little freckle-faced bundle of Americana, Amy Carter (the miniature white hope?). I was scared for myself. Doing music and words all over again after nearly six months of silence. Except that this wasn't going to be an eight-piece r & b band backing me up, but one man with the equivalent power of most space-age orchestras, and then some—

I was terrified I wouldn't be up to it. We had rehearsed only once before and that was last month in California; this was Indianapolis and things had changed. Ideas had changed, enthusiasm had changed, even our bodies had changed. I had been in the sun for a week and swam in the Pacific ocean and watched dolphins dance in private pools just to get myself in gear for this moment—a morning where snow gently showered down a still, dark city. The Indianapolis Museum of Modern Art is the kind of place where they still deem it necessary to have voices booming over the loud-speaking system: "We hope you are enjoying the exhibits, but please do not touch the works of art."

The man who put the concert together is a poet named Ron Wray. He is a good friend of Etheridge Knight, who I wished would suddenly show up and create some cheerful madness in this joint. It is Ron Wray's birthday, which I think is a good omen.

Roscoe and I were the works of art on display that afternoon at the museum. Museums make me nervous. They remind me of tombs tastefully decorated by Bloomingdale's. Even the Louvre has a musty, imposing smell. One time Ntozake Shange and I flew down to Pasadena to read at the museum of modern art there, which is very expensive-looking and dreadfully modern, and I was really impressed by all these old literary ladies in attendance and the money that had obviously been sunk into all those abstract sculptures and minimalist paintings. Zake bought an African necklace in the bookshop and that's about all I remember about that strange afternoon. I think I vowed to never read at a museum of modern anything again. But that's another story.

Ron had worked really hard to get a grant so we could perform at the Indianapolis museum. I had backed out of my commitment a couple of times already, but finally, after much heartburn and misgivings, decided to go ahead with the project. They had warned us that there might not be a large audience because so many people who wanted to hear us would be intimidated by going to the museum. "Oh, shit," I groaned, "we shoulda been booked into a nightclub or something..."

To our pleasant surprise, the large room was filled with people, with folks even sitting on the floor. Old people, young people, would-be musicians and regular musicians and poets; it was lovely. After the performance, the questions came fast and furious from this eager, enthusiastic audience...

A young blonde man (who looked like the young blonde man from Michigan who asked me if I was Jessica Hagedorn at the train station in Oslo—I wasn't sure) asks me a convoluted question about my poem "Easter Sunday." All I can focus on is his phrase "lysergic consciousness"—something about the lysergic consciousness he says is inherent in my poem. He was apparently being sweet and sincere, and I didn't feel like responding with the usual condescension one reacts with during a lot of pointless "discussions."

A million thoughts were zooming through my mind. It was time to get off my ass and get back to the words and the music. This day had been evidence that I could still do it, and do it in new ways: with an eight-piece band, with solo guitar or solo saxophone, with two green parrots perched on my shoulder, or all alone. All alone! That was the most satisfying realization of all.

A musician in the audience raises his hand. He asks me if I've ever done "anything with the entire Art Ensemble of Chicago." I smile. (I got beautiful Bugs Bunny teeth and I feel radiant smiling.) "Yeah," I say, beaming down on him with all the sunshine I can muster up from the South Pacific, "I've had dinner with them a few times..."

JESSICA HAGEDORN

My need for trouble. After all the good news, the doctor's "everything that was there is gone"—all the months of fear and chemicals, diarrhea and sharp pains, veins closing and opening, and now the news is "good", a small word "good", and I don't know how to feel. Mark brings flowers home, Kathy brings flowers, friends call and tell me I must be dancing with glee.

I am only glad. Worried. Like after I finished the cancer poem I knew it was the best thing I had done, but when I heard they would make a chapbook I was worried. Will this raise false hopes, false opinions? Am I now really that good a poet? Those high lyric moments that came from the crucible, the *bright light of shipwreck* George calls it, nothing like that will happen. And everyone will expect me to be a poet and all I did was write a poem. "Congrats on your chapbook" Karen wrote, and Mark telling all his friends, and me worried. The next the next the next things?

Same now, all are thrilled and I'm worried. Will there be more tumors, what about that dream, all the bugs getting loose in the house. All the rejoicing going on around me and I'm numb, I know I'm still anxious, I worry about everything. I can't bear to listen to the news, drought, storm, and I think "my sons, what will happen to the economy who will come to a night club who will pay for documentaries who will buy paintings, turn it off what will happen to my sons?" This worrying will get more tumors, why can't I simply simply rejoice?

What would happen to me if I were REALLY well? Would everyone stop loving me? Who would dance around in circles if I hadn't been sick first, and so dramatically? In my poem: *what about love/ my mother says I think you're catching cold/ of course I love you.* If the poems are really good will that engender love or only admiration? How to know in my deep bones that sympathy is not love? Gratitude is not love? Envy is not love? Pity is not love? Sex is not love? Staying alive is love. Staying alive is love!

FRANCES JAFFER

The Father Story

He was. I am. He was. Becoming a father. How do you. Become.
Belly round. Rounder. Hand. *Kick. Hand. Kick.* Cactus.
The fear there. *Pin. Prickle.*

He was not. A young man. Or an old one. The culture
said. Barren. He was barren. Barren until. Until he was.
He was not. Actually. He had been a bird. No. He had not.
He had just been. Up there.

He did not. Drive an ambulance. Into it. He wasn't
even bandaged. When it finally happened. Naked. Naked.
The grove was red. Bare. Madrone. The skin smooth trunks.
The bark pealing. Fed him.

I went into the woods. Wood. The sap cleft to my chest.
It was. Sticky there.

I could no longer look. For my own father. Or fly.
From my mother.

The truth was in a low sound. *Birrr. Birrr.* Not
cold. Just the.

    I came to. A tuba. In my own. Throat.
    I went. Intestine. *Laby. Rinth. Laby.*

Down there. In. There. A. Home. A whistle. A.
   Going home. Coming out.
The place. The boundary.

    He met the animal. There. tore him.
Down. Way. Far. He came up. Not a.
Father. No. He did not. He came up.
The seed ball. Bursting.

    Fatherhood. Resting. In the branches. A nest.
Force of the trunk. Spoken.
Come home. My child. It is me. Father
me. I love you. Father. Me. I will.

STEPHEN VINCENT

Sixth Month

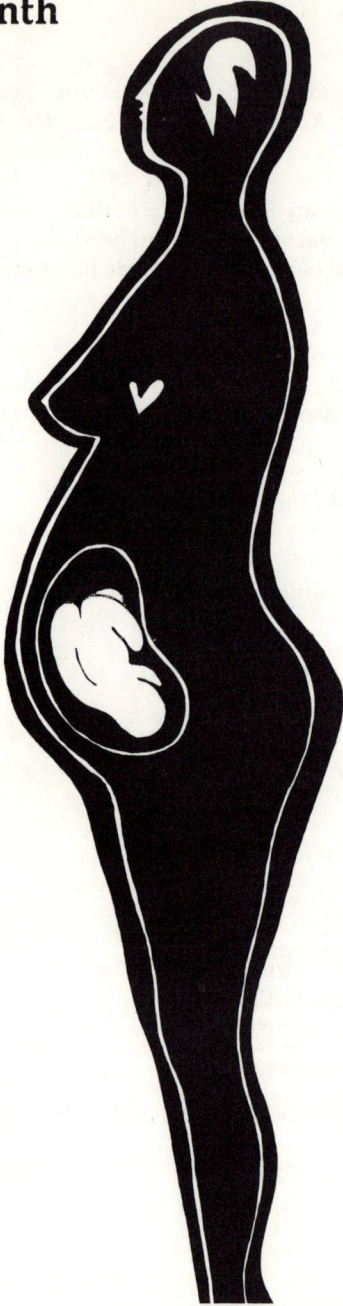

DEBRA McGEE

Bionic Booties

Groceries & toilet bowl cleaner
followed by a profound vacuuming of
hall rug runway & then routine
folding of sheets & shirts out of the drier
also yelling at the kids to clean dog shit
& yelling at humiliating food stamp workers
then supper & near hysterical laugher
& a lifetime of coffee & Danish
& making the bed then cleaning the tub
& rushing the day to a photo-finish
in hot steamy water, wanting only just to get
a handle on all this detail
or at least a budget
then kiss & make up
as we sleep in our arms of a soft & startling routine
worked up by worries & getting sticky against our bodies
& wake up to cornflakes & the kids
as they laugh at their Bionic Booties
doing the bump with that big fat
McBreakfast—
  "Hey they dragged a
dead body outta the projects—overdose"—
in a land where the Fonz meets Bruce Lee in his Bens
eating adobo burritos & the slick images cover up a real power
we can only indicate how to take
knowing it's up to them to internalize & make firm—
"Why we so poor when we work so hard?"—
so we kick them out shrieking to school
as others get kicked out too
& early morning the sidewalk fills up
with dozens of beautiful bad kids half Apache half Oakie
half Filipino half Jewish half Black half Chicano
like a new nationality called
the Mission District of SF

HILTON OBENZINGER

Two headlines from the front page of the *San Francisco Chronicle*:

"Carter's CIA Findings—
Nothing 'Illegal, Improper'
Secrecy Defended"

"Digging Into Your Family's History"

This is about secrets and walking over old ground. This is about the story of anyone's life—which is a dream. In the dream "a number of strangers" appear. They "always signify 'a secret.'" In anyone's life a number of strangers appear. They are walking.

She spoke of the novel. She said there was "a front story" and a "back story." The "front story" is the dream. It is a mythical country. A "front." A facade. The face we put on.

The "back story" is history. Anyone's life. Secrets. It is opaque. It is as dark and public as a newspaper headline.

This is about newspaper headlines and history. Which is a secret.

Which is a secret?

Is this about anyone's life: Which is a secret?

BEVERLY DAHLEN

This morning I call up that prick Abel & get the runaround about how the property has to go through escrow before I get paid the measly $38 they owe me. They can't find the bill. Send them another one, certified. I should have been warned when that classic scrawny Okie on the job told me he hadn't been paid. "Well," I said, on the way to the dump, "no problem getting paid." I was thinking of small claims court. "Yeah," he said, "I'll just get another job," using some kind of superior Okie Zen logic. I guess it's hard to file a small claims suit when you don't have any money or an address. Luckily I got the name of the painters there, just in case I needed witnesses for the future, which I bet I will. Since I'm cleaning my desk & coming up with such turkeys as Abel, I dutifully try to figure out a way to expand my book of poems for George. Old poems in back? I try. Nope. George is just going to have to make do with the 80 odd pages of ERASE WORDS; too bad, George, another slim volume of poems, the publisher's bane. Another reason I'm cleaning my desk is because I've finished the 2nd half of my novel, *Percy Q*. It was a pleasure to kill off over 15 poets & an unspecified number of English teachers. Such are the rewards of writing fiction. I've got to: read the material for the Nevada PITS program; check the garden for wind damage; draft a letter to Aloha Lei; clean up letter file; just writing those things down makes me hate them. I refuse to do any of them. I think about call girls instead. The Chronicle's so helpfull for wasting time. I think about Dave Kopay (a childhood hero) saying that he peddled his ass to executives when he was a football player. If I only knew what depths a simple love of mashing male bodies with plastic pads all over my body would lead to, I'd have never accepted that free ride to college. I thank my lucky stars I was thrown out for drinking early in my career. I could have ended up just like Dave Kopay: free white gay & thirty-ish and completely unemployable in the rugged man's world of football. So instead I'm free white hetero and thirtyish and completely unemployable in the rugged man's world of American poetry. Perhaps I should review the career of James Dickey. And I certainly didn't end up on the sports page of the Chronicle telling my life story. I ended up on Omens telling my life story. I wonder what everyone else is writing about? The butchering in Uganda? Wait until some sharp NY art dealer gets ahold of Amin in exile and ships him to the US a la King Kong & books him at all the parties there. I can just hear Art Forum now: "The variegated tension created by the bilateral sweeping gestures of the dictator inculcates bifurcating tensions in the viewer where the bicameral emotions of life and death, art and life, effect an indeterminate inordinate binomial act of mind, leading to the piece de resistance of Amin's performance: hanging by his heels over a puddle of simulated blood."

Keith Abbott

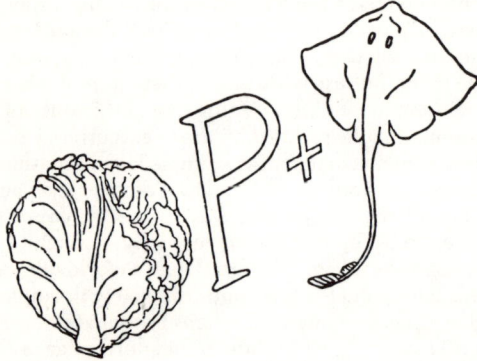

Michael Myers

Plains, Georgia
February 26, 1977

Hello, My Pal,

Wouldn't you know trouble don't end? You get a drop of rain, a little sun, then *bang!* comes out of nowhere this giant-size living cracker nightmare over in Uganda, oooh, he's a mean balloon! Miz Lillian, she wants to suit up in her Peace Corps suit and shoot on over, teach him manners and his living wives manners and his chirren. Like hell. For all we know ole cigarface Fidel already give Idi nukes and he like to blow us all to Kingdom Come. It's not funny, brother. Everybody be getting nukes next. Chad. Botswana. Ifni. Delaware. (Just kidding.) Be having us a nuke free-for-all, and no amount of beer ever going to make us happy again. I heard the other day, some scientist, he said we just like a pea floating in space all set to sooner or later collide with some other pea. I know it. You know it. We got it writ down inside, in the program. If it's in the program, it could make us crazy. No lie. This planet going to bang into some other planet, some meteorite, some star, some lost piece of sun, some something someday, maybe even before some somebody like Idi blow off a nuke. No wonder I been sleeping poorly.

My best to you,

Billy Carter

P.S.—Jimmy been sleeping poorly, too.

A Novel

Out of the city at last, Susan and I are visiting the Banghorn's in the town of _____, where we have a drink in the yard. While David finishes putting molding onto a living room wall, Catherine turns over an irregular border to the garden and talks with us.

She tosses out a length of garden hose, arranges it attractively, then spades on one side only. Catherine is beautiful, looking like a work of art which instead of being painted by El Greco has been photographed by Dorothea Lange.

It's going to rain so we toss some grass seed on the unspaded side, dig a few bulbs in the edges of the border, and go into the house.

A piece of molding crosses the dining room and lies in David's hands on a power-saw bed. David has a theologian's beard. I recollect a student, closely resembling him, who served donuts in the basement lounge of the department of religion's building, ten years ago at the University of X.

Once the student put a question to a famous theologian, just ahead of me in the line for sweets and coffee. "How can every act be holy?" A 'zen' christian, the theologian actually held the view that all human activities, whether so intended or not, were sacred. Becoming conscious of this fact, one might lead a totally religious life and attain knowledge of God.

The student must not have been asking for moral advice. More probably his question was intended to be theoretical. In any case, I didn't hear the theologian's answer, if any. In a moment he had departed towards a table on the other side of the lounge where several students awaited him, their chairs pushed back to face the direction from which he walked, pastry and beverage in his hands.

Soon the chairs closed back around the table. My attention was diverted by a jelly-filled donut, and I recall no more of the incident.

I must be thinking about it today in connection with the President's "personal Morality", so much in the news. The people would not wait for Moses and worshipped a golden calf. Moses armed them one against another and, as Exodus relates, "there fell of the people that day about 3000 men" (32;28).

Susan seeded longest in the rain, and has been drying her hair.

Now she comes back into the room. David has finished the living room. He and Catherine are going to change, then we will drive into town for a drink.

Waiting, I listen to a violin and, behind it, hear the radio making the violin's sound and its own, behind which David and Catherine are coming out of their room. Behind their sounds are street sounds, the facing houses sounding, the streets and houses behind them—down to the Pacific in constant sound. The last few days I have been reading Edmond Jabes. I have become crazed with questions.

TOM MANDEL

28

Parting Waves

There was so much to be said when the night split in two
You said conflict destroys our relationship
Have you noticed Silence kills it too?

With arms clinging to one another two
Bodies glide through the grey pottage of
The morning. Walking on yellow sands
That will never be captured in a glass
Vial; they walk. The sands flow.

Already I know only memories of you
Even while you populate the same room
Your taciturn, your reticence—A slander
My feathers are scattered. They lay
Around your feet like flicked ashes.

The sands stretch out miles and miles
They walk making pock marks
On the shore—promising return. Slowly
The waters approach. Slowly the sands fill
The sunken pits turning them smooth;
No tracks, no back glances, no regrets.

Quietly I'll leave. Only fools hang like
Spanish moss. I know somehow isolation
Burned like acid in the unwanted tranquility
When the need for changes are felt. But swiftly I'll go.
Absence will be an eclipse of our love
That shown moon full and brilliant.

The sea advanced, retracted like a beckoning muse
Searching and searching for a new love. They stood in
Attention as the sun arched in the horizon slowly
Ascending, opening a sleepy red eye. The waves
Benevolently rushed, tumulted and broke above their heads.

JOSELYN IGNACIO

1

Ernesto Cardenal Comes To The Mission

Human rights Carter waves $= Arms formula to tropical dictators sunning themselves & drinking Coke. Cable received by visiting Nica poet at Channel 20 STOP Carter may stop military aid to Somoza STOP

Ernesto Cardenal comes to exorcise the spirit of capitalism, the spirit of imperialism, of Somocism & ego from the babies and children of our barrio—he brings communion w/ the people The old men w/ memories of a distant land and an ancient struggle come to hear Ernesto. Fresh eyed children and the rest of the pueblo comes out to hear and see the poet-priest (Cultural Worker)

A man like any man you see walking down Mission St. puts an arm around Ernesto and tells the other Nicas gathered around him "Tho you may not believe it—this man is a prophet." They already believe it. They already know.

The people listen to Ernesto when he reads about the death of Leonel Rugama in a poor barrio of Managua and they laugh when he mocks Somoza and they become concerned when finally at the end he reads, *La LLegada,* No one knows anymore if Ernesto will ever return or what fate awaits him in Nicaragua.

Carter backs down from the human rights issue because in the end he favors $ and its ways or because he prefers gorilla dictators to communilism.

And Ernesto Cardenals goes back to Nicaragua. When will he return to the Mission?

ALEJANDRO MURGUIA

The rain is falling
red at the windows, yellow, purple, green
do you see it crosses whatever one is doing
that is a triumph of the weather
no language is without its sun and storms
now it is hailing
under the command of my imagination
my last freedom
everything is obscure and remains
everything remains to be learned
we look at the cans on the shelf
and the tablecloth shaken clean
the dog is an obstacle in the room
you spoke of pianos and I of horses
are attached to the colors
of the imagination
so it seems in some directions
obscurity is a thing of freedom
your life is no longer a show
to be named
no one is caught like a finger
now let's retain whatever mystery we have
the wings of a plane are paddling the sky
in the shine of the storm
there are cruel and poor men and women
and others like saints at their counters
today everyone is dressed
no one watches the street
everyone glances along the sidewalk
I am pursuing Wednesday while it rains
under the command of my imagination

LYN HEJINIAN

Carlos Bulosan:
Pilipino poet

carlos bulosan   but lasting no more   pilipino poet   than a split second

carlos bulosan
pilipino poet

but lasting no more
than a split second

the manong's held you
down to the old cot

the first and last embrace
of a naked pilipino man
and chicana woman

unbuckled
your leather belt

brown arms clinging
around each other

that kept
your thin tb body

breathing

together

hot summer sweat

yanked off your pantalon
and then retreated

but it ended

because
it held nothing

in the background
of music and card playing

but a zero
in a pocket

left your naked body
lying there alone

of erections

trembling with a woman

like a sweet dream
inside a warm opening

you kept
the cries down

gone away

for only a moment

remembering nothing
but the words

wiping the pain away
releasing the milky sap

of the woman

in pure savage-brown ecstasy

"do you like it?"
"do you like it?"

AL ROBLES

AIR CORPS TECHNICAL SCHOOL
KEESLER FIELD, MISSISSIPPI

THE SWISS GUARDS

are the more amusing
squeezed in one of two books
read for keeps

tracking profits
opposite to free enterprise
in moscow news is slower

moves into an earthquake
only instruments felt
lighter at both ends

g.e. lightbulbs for an addict, one dollar
pneumatic shoes
just have an idea

missionary imperialism
lady churchill
is not poor

sell the china dogs
bankrupt countries
money for old oil

must be cheapened

TOM RAWORTH

All These Examples

'You know, in Georgia, we all learned Latin.' *the President*

This the quick halibut's so rusty
so's a piece
jab-jobs
knocks rue it, no header am spared it
Sir Witzio, e.g., crossed finder-hairs and
one dead halibut   o and
shoulder it, center upon the shoulder
ante trivial   monday pringles
tu(taterpops)esday   genuisti filium
teacup in   wednesday's rain
on donnerstag two dogs   halibut traces in fog

my friend with the long nose and strides
is an appreciative person resisting thought
'a work of 18 years fishing'
in these waters: no doubt many molecules the same
of fishers and farmers. Came out the house in Lans
the day we left, to find the elder Ravix on the path
asking had we seen his cow (famous for escaping).
The son had been to school in Lyons: there were
milking machines & in back the old stalls. The old man
appreciated that; he showed me his hands
                                        warning me to
drink quickly on such stormy days—anyway their faces
pure slav like their name, yet the town cemetary revealed
stones back five centuries named Ravix.

This is the Latin peasant stock straight back to Eastern Invasions.
Farmers and fishers: for several years these spectra
will dwarf the two men, resisting thought, advancing in the bus
longer and longer these same bowls grow white
and in the forefront a phalanx of seven. 'Step
right this way, I'll make you a farmer of men.'

TOM MANDEL

President Jimmy Carter and wife Rosalynn Carter
Israeli Prime Minister Yitzhak Rabin and wife Leah Rabin
Stand at attention upon a reviewing stand on the White House Lawn
They stand with eyes raised and hands on heart
As if in the presence of multitudes.
But before them only a four man color guard
stands at rigid attention on the deserted lawn.

DAVID HENDERSON

Mastercharge

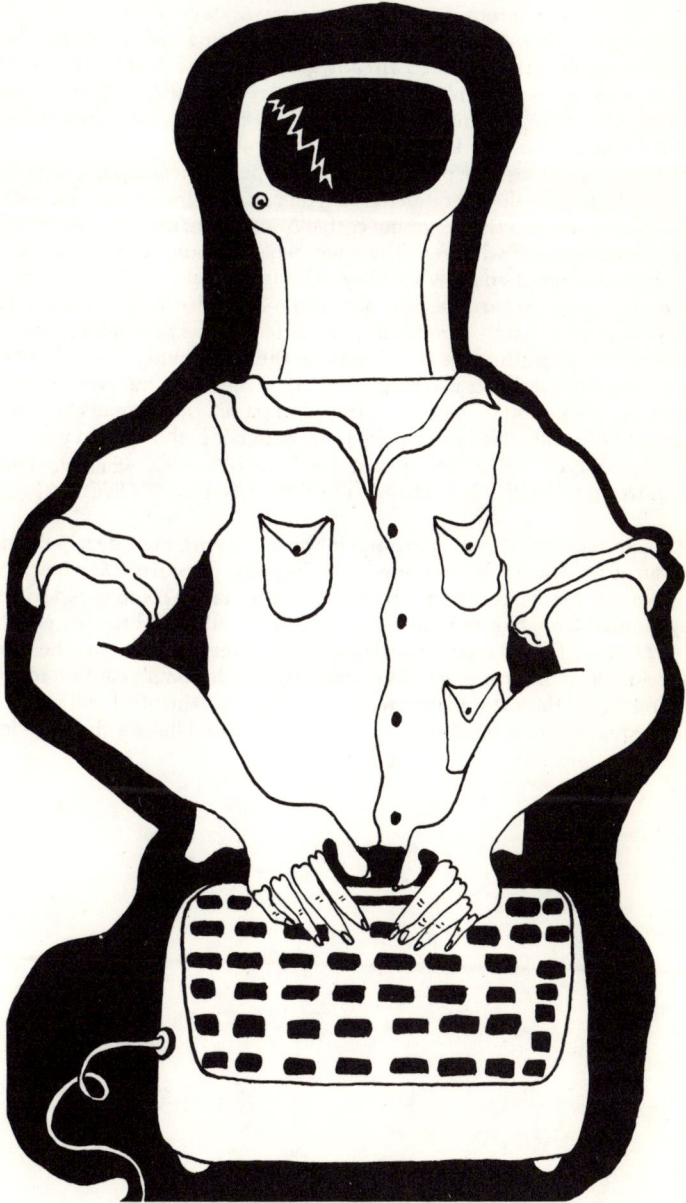

DEBRA McGEE

Putting On A Show

what a coincidence. international women's day & steve picks me to do the day book. actually, a great day—spent hours of it demonstrating against the mitchell brothers' sicko show at the ultra room. i'd already gone there & asked him to lay off, & talked to the women working there; no result; so today there were 100 of us. marching, picketing, chanting—gabbing with the press, & our pals, who dropped by on their lunch hour just cause they knew what a party it would be. the employees bringing us coffee ("hope you close the place down."), the performers talking with us, ("dont lose our jobs for us—just get it better, if you can.") & i wear out fast—sit in the lobby for minutes at a time, sipping coffee & watching the press wander in & out, listen to artie mitchell whining, "these women arent stupid. they picked goddamn international woman's day, when they're bound to get female reporters"—& i sat there & sipped coffee & rubbed my sore feet—i wonder if there's an age past which when you go on a march, you need more coffee breaks than march time. listening to the women inside putting on a show so that the men could play with themselves in their comfy circle jerk—& listening, too, to the script the men wrote for those women: "comeon, bitch! it's *your* turn to feel pain!" the woman being beaten screaming while the other woman hits her. & outside, the women who can afford pride, chanting 2-4-6.8.10. we are not the slaves of men! & whenever i go out there, i want us to sing, HAPPY WOMAN'S DAY TO US, HAPPY WOMAN'S DAY TO US—

jennifer stone trudging around in the circle with me, "dear, why dont we see if we can get a little more free coffee? maybe some popcorn?" & when a man asks are we dykes, she looms over him, "are you my alternative?" many old friends there; many women who, like me, have retreated from public politics for years, trying to sew our lives to fit our needs, now back on the streets demanding the changes that must be made in order for us to live. thinking of alice paul's cautionary remark: "stop fretting with the tar babies. without the e.r.a., this stuff will go on & on. if we *had* the equal rights amendment, those women would have a choice of jobs!"

He tipped the Oly up to the blue
& polished it off.
I steered the beat up Caddy
away from ruts & he
flung the can out the window
into a confusion of manzanita & oak & second growth

"Ya know why I did that?"
he asked, like a bark.
"Uh no, why?"
"Cause this is *my* land
& I can do any goddam thing I *want*
on *my* land!"
& then his anger subsided.

What's his he'll take, unashamed, like
spotlight a deer, blind it & blow it away.
"Yer a printer, Print me
a bumper sticker says:

I'm a Yurok Indian & I'm proud & you can take your goddam white man's religion back over the ocean where it came from & shove it

Sometimes anger & hope & shame spun together
can get longer than a 65 Caddy bumper.
He's been saying the same things for years.
It explodes, tears through imported Scottish weed
& Himalaya berries, goes crazy.
Original redwood has been cleared for
long rows of sublets in San Jose
& the 2nd growth is unruly & a tangle.

Being white & in endless supply
I need to check my own panic
or my own paternal winks.
He don't know all the answers
except his—
& even those don't come with instructions
on how to assemble
an authentic model of a nation.

He's been saying it for years:
*"We are the evidence of this
Western Hemisphere."*
We swerve down the road, him
pulling out his 38
taking pot shots at beehives
& laughing it up.

HILTON OBENZINGER

the leopard

once undressed
yr markings are displayed
with elegance
the languid dance
before you execute
yr prey

as if i didn't know
i was the kill
yr tongue
camouflaging growls
with a kiss

in costume
you casually join
the crowd
gaping at museum walls
oohing and ahhing
with the best of them

you slip a hand
into my dress
tenderly fondling
each breast
as if i didn't know
about those claws
pulled back
inside the fur.

Vulva Operetta: in my dream, sweaters are referred to as "vulvas." They
are mohair or angora wool, of a soft warm texture. We wear these
"sweaters." They are all the same colors—gray, bleeding into a deep blood
red. Similar to Japanese Raku pottery.
People say things like, "it's hot . . . I think I'll take my vulva off." Or, "It's
cold . . . I think I'll put my vulva on." Foppish men and women ask each
other things like, "Where did you get that beautiful vulva?" followed by
remarks like, "I'm gonna put my vulva in the closet."

JESSICA HAGEDORN

Michael Myers

from aRb

Thus it is essential that for Saussure's tree and Lacan's door we substitute

as the prototypical model for the equation S/s, in which it is the function of the signifier (S) which brings the *possibility* of the object in all its dimensions into view (here problematized by that ambivalence characteristic of multistability and even conceivably a language-specific example not to be repeated in cultures which have no such general category as the cubic), a signifier which by its very nature is the proposition of an ideal object, not a reflection of the twelve connected straight lines upon a plane which constitutes here the signified (s). Hence Derrida may be read as a map of the bar (/) within this algorithm of the sign. Yet his idealism violates his own truth: that *alterity alters.* The origin of language, of writing, which is the origin also of the *tool*, constitutes the whole of the possibility of history and society, and they in turn alter and determine that of language, of writing. So that into society is brought forward a dialectic whose originary mode is that double helix of deoxyribonucleic acid, the one cell in nature privileged to reduplicate, to *other*, itself, tending always toward more adaptive forms, now vastly problematized by the transformation from biochemistry into history, to the point where the increasingly rapid evolution of material life threatens the very adaptive capacity of the genes of humankind to respond: alterity alters, ad infinitum. And the text is none other than the very fact of our lives.

RON SILLIMAN

Plains, Georgia
March 12, 1977

Hello My Pal—
    You asked what's been happening. Here's what: Jimmy
saw Tut. (No lie.) He went on down to the museum where
they showing the ole sub-Ra King's coffin and treasures.
People was lined up outside, waiting in the wind. Jimmy cut
right on past. Inside there was bronze and jewels, semi and
precious, and unwrapped mummies. There was sceptres and
stones. Implements. Bones. Dust everywhere. The air
smelled like Egypt, like sun-warmed sand. (I dreamed it
smelled like Egypt.) (I been dreaming bad again.)
    Then Jimmy saw Tut. He saw a Tutface carved on the
coffin. In the photo in the paper Jimmy's own face looks still
and carved, like he felt Tut looking back at him from way
back yonder in the deep corridor of what is remembered, history. Jimmy looks still and cold. Or maybe he was only
posing. He been doing that lately, getting twisted into rare
shapes. Sometimes when I catch his image quick off a surface
as it comes to me through that second lens I don't recognize
him at all. Imagine, me his brother and the captured face like
a blank to me.
    Power is dust. Forms need filling. Coffins fit tight.
    Now I earned a beer.
    Anyhow, pal, Jimmy saw Tut and Tut saw Jimmy and
what got exchanged is a long dark secret. See, all I know's
what I read in the papers: papers said on his way out Jimmy
told the lined-up people waiting in the wind that the wait
would be well worth it.

Best to you,

Billy Carter

Huge thick braided rain early a.m., bikes in the alley wet again, dream that all my work is like a clay bear's head I have to carry around which keeps falling apart. Procrastinating over my longpoem, heard screams, a couple up the street having a fight, they smashed their cars together, he kept driving off & coming back, she would hit him & then he drove another 10 feet and stopped, from our distance Jan & I had to laugh, reminded of our own terrible times. Finally he started the truck and with a beautiful move she hoisted herself into the back of the pickup and they drove off like that. In the longpoem my narrator is trying to decide whether or not to go to a world I know she'll decide to go to but never get there. Jan & kids went rollerskating at a rink rented for Pisces party. Karla came to visit, once the baby next door, once my child-lover, strange to see someone I'd known so long and not seen for 10 years, a luminous fused conversation of redis-covery. She's a weaver living in a craftpersons community in Delaware Water Gap National Park. We talked of generations, rainmagic, losing & finding ourselves, work, knowledge, apocalypse; shared tea and smoke and love with words & eyes across a certain space and at 2 o'clock she was gone again for 3000 miles. Family back bushed, Jan to Med to write her paper, Kia and Zoe play in backyard (they are famous named Jennie and Jennifer), I went running & meditated to still my mind's agitation, typing up children's poems, grouching at everyone—("why is the sea blue?/ why am I sitting here?/ why am i getting old?"—Diedre, grade 4) now Jan starts reading THE LITTLE HOUSE IN THE BIG WOODS, my whole family sitting on the bed with long legs & brown hair & primate fingers, the cat too a feature-less ball of gray fur, "leaves & flowers & stars, crescent moons & curlicues," precious, vulnerable. Karla said "it just keeps going, over and over," and I said we never would see a resolution, not unless we're the last humans on the planet, then we would.

JOHN OLIVER SIMON

RENE YANES

I wake up in the a.m. with a searing dry throat. The heat is on and in this little box of a room it's completely dry. Outside it is snowing. My throat is aching. I wonder how the fuck you can keep warm and still breathe. There's no clock, no phone, no TV, no radio. This room comes equipped with a bed. Be thankful. I watch the snow and then the sun rising over the hills. After it gets above the bottom power line, I think it must be time. As I walk into town I notice that the white ski cap is still frozen in the same place alongside the road. No one's been walking into town since it snowed. A car goes by. I've noticed that they don't let their cars warm up here. So they start off sounding like vacuum cleaners: phoooooooooomlp-poop-phooooop. I wonder why they don't let them warm up. I'm early. Tomorrow morning I'll wait until the sun gets up above the second power line. In my 3-4th grade class the teacher has the curtains drawn against the sun, the windows open because of the sun and the heaters, and it's still stifling. My throat gives out and I find myself wishing they had a teacher's room in this school so I could make myself a cup of ginseng, the only thing for a sore throat. I go up one block to the main drag and get some cough drops between classes. I'm the first poet they've had up here in Virginia City. The main entertainment is the high school basketball team. It was a little disconcerting to read the bumper stickers the first day: VC POWER, VC PRIDE, VC #1. VC is still Viet Cong to me. After teaching 7-8, 9-10, & Senior English, I go back to the Sugar Loaf Motel and take a nap. I wake up just as it's getting dark. I hike in to The New Sharon House and the bartender and I talk. He tells me about his fused spine and how his girlfriend babysat his dope plants while he was in the hospital and got busted. When the Brady Bunch comes on the color TV, I go have Almond Duck. The chef here is incredible. I lurch back in the bar and have an Irish coffee. I'm going to try to stay up as late as I can so I don't wake up at 3 a.m. again. The bartender floats a little creme de cacao on top of the whiskey in the Irish & I like it better that way. File for future drinking. I feel like staying but I'm too full & sleepy. I walk outside and the freezing weather wakes me up. I walk about 2 blocks & decide I'd rather walk 4 blocks back to my motel with the wind than 2 blocks back to the bar against it. Footprints around the frozen ski cap. I think about how incredible it was that this shell of a town once had 30,000 people. Nothing but terraces and a few old houses now. I read Walt Whitman & think about 19th Century America. I fall asleep forgetting to turn down the thermostat. I wake up in the a.m. my throat burning. I drink two glasses of water & open the window. I'll freeze but at least I'll be able to breathe until I do. Gradually I fall asleep. I dream a lovely dream & wake up freezing. I close the window & write it down as the snow falls outside in the darkness.

KEITH ABBOTT

The Death of a Cat

March 16. A week ago cat Belisa died. For ten years she was near the centers of my life. My ex-wife Maria once complained that I was more affectionate to the cat than to her. Then Karen resented the cat at first, eventually came to love her as much as I did. Perhaps Karen became more affectionate to the cat than to me.

Belisa had run away because we filled the house with children, a Sunday family gathering. When she came back Tuesday afternoon she was aloof, not unusual, and very quiet. In the middle of the night she woke us with her violent retchings. She spent the rest of the night in terrible convulsions, rejecting any attention or comfort we tried giving her. Between convulsions she gravitated nose-first into the corners of our bedroom, panting fiercely.

We planned getting her to Doc Hauge at 7:00 AM. About 6:00, while Karen took a bath, Belisa finally came onto the bed to see me, collapsing by my side and seeming, for a moment, to rest more easily. Then she struggled off the bed into a corner. I got up and went to the bathroom. When I returned she was stretched out long in the warm hollow I'd left in the bed, her body still retching against the poison, dead.

Karen and I struggled with our feelings of grief. She was a *cat*, after all. We were full of guilt. Why didn't we pay closer attention, figure out much sooner that she'd been poisoned? In the garden one morning I turned and saw Belisa running around the corner of the house. I mentioned it to Karen, and she said that she'd seen her twice the day before, racing in a circle around the house. It was as if her spirit were struggling to free itself, to fly off the edge of this circle, the center of which was somewhere inside our house.

Today as I worked on a wiring project beside the house, Belisa ran behind me. Before she went out of my vision I saw the urgent energy centered in her perfectly white chest as she ran. I turned the other way to follow her flight, and a small white moth zig-zagged in front of me, smoothly rode the wind upwards through the bare branches of the box elder, and disappeared over the house next door.

TOM SCHMIDT

what if Jimmy Carter came to spend the night at my house? boggles. this house is not part of America, can't be. anyway no place for him to sleep/ the floor/ or share backhouse bed with the homeless 18-year-old poet who's ready to start a race war. Kia pinched me this morning because I wasn't wearing green/ at the table of bluebirds cutting out collages "New York is across the world" . . . low day with a sore throat, teaching linebreaks, cooking, adding my enchiladas to the gross National Product . . . got a letter from Pancho in the hole, they confiscated the hawk feather I sent him, afraid he'd fly away on it (smile) . . . his memory image of himself surrounded by guns in the ceremony of weed, escaped . . . "above the treetops a woman sang a glorious song/ take me along if you love me/ take me along if you do/ my heart will sing sweet glorious/ I am of the moon"—Kia . . . Mr. President, please reinstate the Folsom Prison Creative Writers' Workshop. And also help to remove the cadmium, mercury, lead from the children's bones & blood "take me along with you if you love me   " not to mention the secret service, they can sleep in the garden between the comfrey and last year's chard and new sweet peas in the sweet mud of our late rain. Jimmy, man, I almost dare to love and respect you (or has the media hyped me?) but thinking the track record of the Presidents of my life I just don't trust you further than I could throw you down, it's that moral responsibility = self-interest, the old protestant equation you proclaimed 20 jan. & I just wonder which end you/we'll finally grab it from, lust in the heart, make do with less, throw the dishwater in the garden (watch for sleeping secret service), the I Ching says PRE-PONDERANCE OF THE SMALL, watch out, I wrestle with the burnt out death mask of New York America while inwardly hoping for some grand reconciliation, Pancho and the President hugging in the sunlight like two smiling flowers, smile, fly away. Irreconcilable human needs. Free the p-oets. Save the children. Beware of spiders in the compost pile, light on the edges of clouds, men in the crowd with a silencer, it's a long spiral road thru the geography of dreams, sleep tight, sir. No harm betide. If you need to piss in the middle of the night the bathroom light's on the wall just past the mirror as you go in, but don't flush needlessly.

JOHN OLIVER SIMON

A dark world. The indirection in Chekhov's dialogue. What they are speaking to. Not one another. Not to each other surely. So there is that distance between them, and at the same time there is the sense of the world falling through, that they lose the world in that distance. In between the spaces of their speech.

Evening.

A fishy day. Piscean and reptilian influences. The moon (what was left of it) disappeared before sunset. I didn't see it go. When it comes again, it will come for the vernal equinox.

Underwater.

All day Debra and I working quietly in separate rooms of the apartment. At the end of it she says: "It was almost like this day didn't exist—do you know what I mean? I was going so fast it was almost like the day didn't exist."

> The moon disappears before sunset. Liver slice.
> Thin. Small enough to go down the throat of.
> The big gray steel fin of. It rides.
> Quietly quietly by. Cutting the waves.
> It dives down. Snuffles the gravel.
> The water raises up to the mainland.
> The islands. Palmtrees. Swing and sway.
> A hula cartoon. Old. Black and white.
> All with stars. The deserted beach.
> From somewhere out in the ocean.

☆ ☆ ☆

> The clock—tch tch—mud mud—with its tongue.
> Machines brrrrrrrrrrrrr. They go around.
> They go around so fast they start to
> swallow everything.

☆ ☆ ☆

> A dog sniffs the bone of the moon.
> He stands and howls.
> Moonbone! Moonbone!
> He served her in another life.

BEVERLY DAHLEN

Love & Arms

when you told me you
were drinking wine alone
and felt the moon
my heart became weighted
and i thought of our distance
and how we built a fortress
between us and hung it up
in the sky
i've quit writing love
poems because they become
your face
so i think about
the wars that go
on and yet cannot
separate that from
thinking about
love and your face
everything seems to be
connected
somehow
like the laborer
connected to the straps of the rich
like the heart
connected to the rump
there is a layer of fat

growing around
my heart
emotions get cushioned there
and smolder
a need to share the fire
becomes even greater
writing poetry is not enough
it fattens the heart, yes
the fire blazes
i read this to you
before the ash
before the dawn
a sweaty hand
will carry a wrench
will sew a stitch
the fire will blaze
a blood union
the connection becomes
clear
the silence and the fortress
will then be a vacuum
in the heart that
ceases to move
when the wind shifts

JOSELYN IGNACIO

The machines that write Carter's personal replies

By James McCartney
Knight News Service

WASHINGTON — In a small room across the street from the White House, an automatic pen bustl... ...Jimmy Carter's signature six days a ...he has never seen.

...t 600 to 1,200 times a week, and ...,000 times since Carter became

...signature machine is in the ...170 employes analyze, classify ...Carter's mail.

...chinery also produces thousands of ...ing printed signatures and "personal" ...from the President.

...ates with 25 or 30 form letters, ...on ...in large numb...

neatly by the automatic pen, "Jimmy Carter."

Or let's say your church is having an anniversary and you write to tell the President about it. A form letter on file reads:

"To the Congregation of (blank):

"Congratulations on the anniversay of your congregation. It is a pleasure to send my very best wishes to all of you and join in your prayers and continued spiritual strength for all Americans.

Sincerely,
Jimmy Carter

A letter already has been prepared for people congratulating Carter on his desire to stay close to the public and who invite him to stay in their h...

...your ...y close

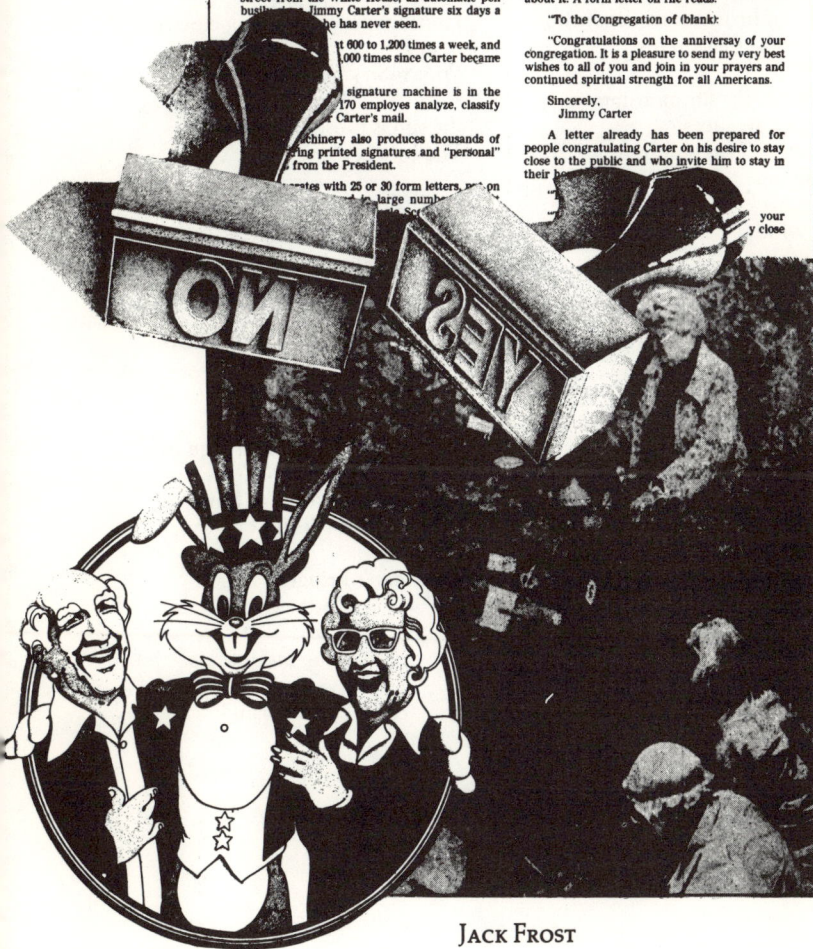

JACK FROST

Poor Man's Bridge/Portsmouth Square

Poor man's bridge
            Portsmouth Square
Forty pine trees scattered
Trimmed and pruned
Dugged out two trees
A few flowers bloom

The pine branches
Cut in and out
Green and brown pine needles
A few horse flies on top

            Persimmon-moon
Three yellow faces
            Two children
On a swing
Swings back and forth
In the wind
Yellow-blue
Thru the trees
Round round faces
Fresh as a thousand autumns

Poor man's bridge
            Portsmouth Square
Pulls down dark shadows
Old men and women sleep
            Spring away

No more children's playground
Empty sand box

Swings lay dead in the wind
Tangled across
The cold icy bars
No legs dangling thru.

Poor man's bridge
            Portsmouth Square
Yesterday
Only yesterday
The children's faces
Twirled thru the wind
Yesterday
Only yesterday
The tiny bodies played
Hopscotch with passing clouds

Poor man's bridge
            Portsmouth Square
the sun is buried underneath
The cold cement

Far gone is the laughter
That grows tall in Spring
Far gone are the old chinese women
With ancient cracked-white
Porcelain faces
Chattering in the long day sun
Far gone is spring

Poor man's bridge
            Portsmouth Square
Six steel girder-branches
Blossoms half-a-block long
Stretching nowhere

Poor man's bridge
            Portsmouth Square
Heavier than ten
            dung mountains

            Dead Spring

AL ROBLES

It is springtime in America, and the cowboy is carrying
his ball and glove. He was born in Alaska, but he grew
up in California. Jump green, he says. What do I know
about falling in love? My wife is a river, forks and all.
I'll tell you, he says, I sold some people my pinto horse
and a week later I drove up by their place and saw his
hide nailed to their barn.

He has painted great lips across his face, even over his
moustache, and whitened the first days of spring. The
apple treees are covered with blossoms. In the bar he
meets Florence once again, she with the milkwhite breasts
and the beer, the skyblue eyes. She is the all-American
floozy with the heart of gold. Ho, and who is she to
shyly turn away? She slides coyly on the red stool and
cups her glass in her lovely hand. I saw it all without
the children. The home run and the round up came again.

Well, and here, she says, a woman becomes a woman when
her hair falls over her bosom.

Lyn Hejinian

a page in progress from **Ency**

Until within nine month the supplementarity cured or dared. To
produce the novelty, the method implored. At one time the regular practice was
this: implored. At one time still incomplete though works, between the proof
practicability out in its ary (still
      longer n in t   it's 31   simultaneous
  's and the thirs   tanedipeden85icaphil appa
          rently in the same spirit   nulamb it volum
ofean
magism   nebyr?   on
                on
          ou   in the co.

      ☆

The sense of familiarity which dwells within
these grounds may finally convince skeptics. In fact,
the peculiar importance attaching to such a work may
finally convince skeptics. Besides it may show a
variety in just this concession. At any conversion,
a visitor unused to loud ticking won't know himself
what he thinks till much later. The simultaneous
awakening friends often feel—they report it—is a
phenomenon of the same nature. Naturally, many are
still waiting. For
here was
expounding as an ordered system
such his way that, if they
the enterprising provision of capital
no longer represent
so many lapse of time
distinct within units
were made so executive conception
if they   if they
d f *g*
bruckner?   widely differ   position sep. or rent
no op. 4-9

TOM MANDEL

☆

The interior rebels use canoes made out of Boa skin.
The oceans are dark. Their waves come in to meet
the canoe and make it work.

☆

STEPHEN VINCENT

RENE YANES

Spoke rims sparkle as they turn on
carruchas cruising 24th St. real
slow. Yellow neon lights of *La
Porinquena* glow like lanterns hung
in the night/wind

I remember scenes from another era
long buried in a cemetery of the
50's
—a falling apart pool hall w/
faded lettering—
—a crumbling st. that crossed a
small town north of somewhere—

Shu-bop shu-bop my baby

ALEJANDRO MURQUIA

In which: I have a strange white dream about a woman in a horse-drawn carriage who is travelling through spring woods. I see the light rippling around her. She is wearing a large hat and a dress with many ruffles and ornaments. She is beautiful; she leans back in the carriage, smiling.

(Is she Madame Bovary or one of George Eliot's characters who slipped in from my conversation with Tamara yesterday?)

(On the freeway today I noticed how many people driving were smiling about something, smiling to themselves. The late afternoon sun was on them, on their faces. We were driving north through Oakland.)

The woman was being driven through a wooded place but later she is in a city at night. I see her get down from the carriage in a wet street; it is a wide street with many large dark buildings. There are lights; they are reflected in the street. She goes up the steps to the opera, I think, or to the theatre. It is certainly a European city; it is certainly someplace I have never seen.

She has a conversation with a man; they sit at a table in a crowded room. It seems to be an upstairs room, a balcony perhaps, in a restaurant or cafe.

I don't know what they talk about. They may talk about gardening. It doesn't seem likely. They have a lively conversation about something. He seems to be much older than she; he is dressed in dark clothes. They each have a glass of cold white wine. I see the glasses, the chilly glaze of moisture on them, the faint yellow wine through it.

Maybe they do talk about gardening; maybe they argue about it.

I lose it; I lose the language. I don't hear what they say.

They talk about gardening, or architecture. They are in the attic of Kelmscott Manor, which Frederick Evans photographed in 1896. It is the attic at Wuthering Heights, perhaps. Now, in this photograph, you sense the space which language can in no way recreate.

They are standing in that room, talking.

They are someplace, talking. We don't hear what they say. They turn, and smile; they drink wine.

Language is as invisible as air.

BEVERLY DAHLEN

Twin Scare

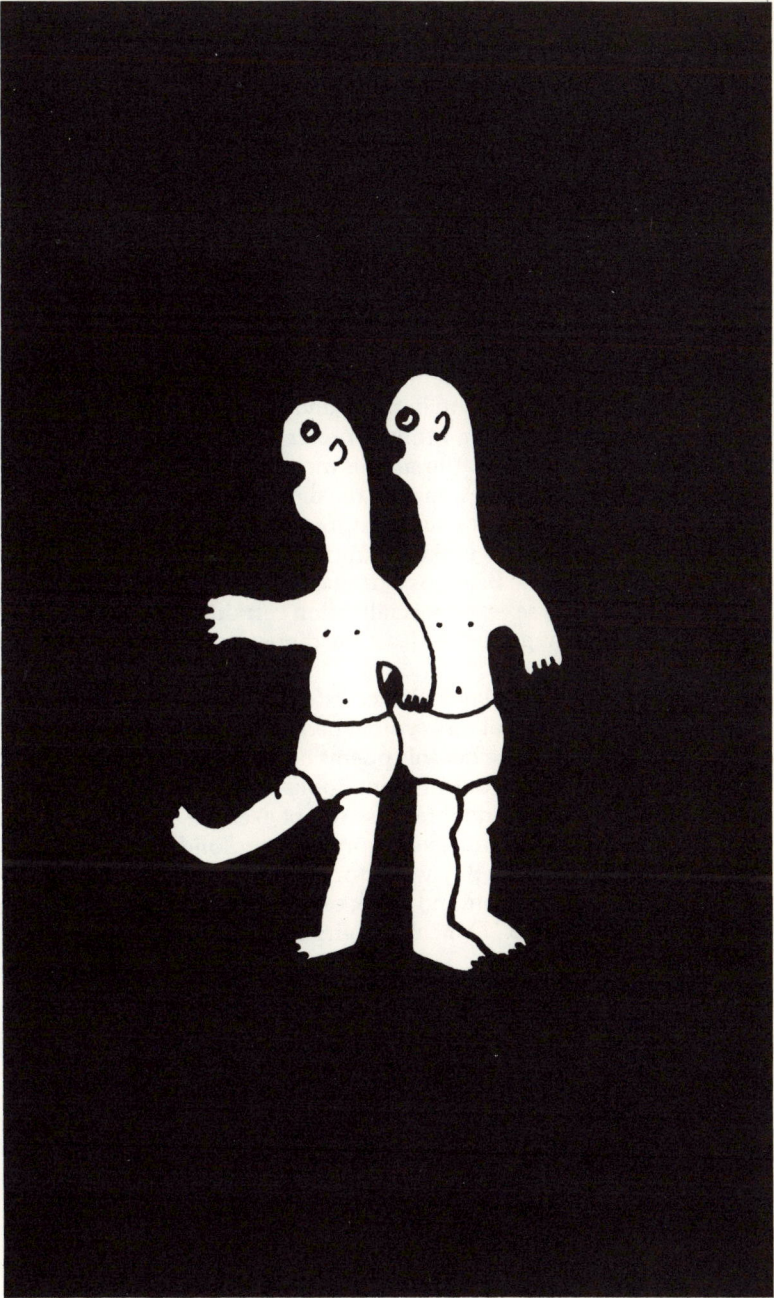

DEBRA MCGEE

Drought:/ come. check the sky the adoration/ is gone, anhydrous the blue world/thickens/   sparkles. cuts. ribbons float downstream, trout struggle. ./ is this the beginning of a poem? I'll work on it tomorrow.

☆ ☆ ☆

Spent the day indoors—another two-day immersion workshop with Diane Di Prima, this time on Robert Duncan. Very different kind of experience from the one on Gertrude Stein—Stein much more a "right-brain" writer. Non-analytical immersion in the sounds of her work yields more for me than in Duncan's. With him, I think I prefer more analysis. He's difficult in a different way. But maybe after all this method is a great jumping-off point for getting into the poems, maybe the difficult ones most of all?

His essays and lectures are exciting. One line I like particularly: "That every gain our specializations make in control and force of our energies is made of the loss of Adamic Being, is a dramatic pathos thruout the creation of the species". Yes, and sex-role specialization certainly led to great "control". Look where it got us! At least the dinosaurs didn't take the whole planet with them.

Sitting two days in the Dance Palace listening to and reading poetry— what an experience! Do the others (young people) take it for granted? Hour-long tapes of the poet reading her/his poems or discussing them—reading aloud ourselves—all Diane's out-of-print books to read from (or xeroxed copies)—acting out plays—and intermissions of exercise, meditation, and lunch to make the concentration even more intense, solid. What a privilege!

Home to a wild Tomales Bay windstorm—house shaking on pilings, cold dry sunset. I wash my hair and drink orange juice (do I think Vitamin C. will resist wind?), read R. Duncan on Virginia Woolf, put potatoes on, wait for Mark to come home.

Francis Jaffer

Liberation of the New Morning Sun

The quiet
blue sky behind
tall trees
The quiet   broken as
she hums
the sun turns to
liquid on her body
she notices moons
on her skin
she hums
the wind joins in
the stream moves   gently
she sits among
fallen leaves
claims them her
children
she hums
the birds wing freely
she thinks of freedom
she picks up her gun
she will join the others

JOSELYN IGNACIO

at the end of the old Mojave Pleiades woman notebook, I dream I have notebooks where I take down every aspect of Poetry In The Schools, notebooks
full of red dust. I drive to the Ridge (burnt-over damp redwood forest,) Sun-
tree shouting at the crossroads, gotta prove we're worthy to live there by
climbing over people's shoulders onto the fire escape while they check our
style, big school board feast with cheese & pie, the cook's negotiating with
Washington for the rest of the meal, everybody sings JINGLE BELLS
making their own verses, I feel out of place, wonder if I'm a city person after
all.

POETRY READING DAY at Washington School, marathon to
10 classrooms with 40 kids reading in all (grades 1-4), scared beforehand
"*I'm* not going to," but contemporaries' respectful attentive silence & laughing applause hooked 'em, Jesse "I didn't know how much fun this was going
to be" (his poem "I want something exciting to happen in my life/ scrambled
eggs are not very exciting/ I want a unicorn in my secret garden") Kia shouting now in the kitchen "told ya told ya told ya never believe" how well she
read, THE GODDESS ("I see her still as stone/ very remote/ flying with
dew in her hair") and Danielle's triumph with the poem of just repeating
MISSISSIPPI down the page I always thot she was being "lazy" and Jim
bowed "thanks for listening to the STAR" and Jenny immediately hit him
with her rolled-up book HARD . . . coulditbe an evil thought that these kids
are right now be/coming P*O*E*T*S?????

begin the new
notebook with Durer in a patch of dandelion, yarrow & skunk-cabbage 400
years ago.

> I breathe these spirits
> the way old Durer drew them
> mud on my fingers,
> grass-stains on my knees

O yes! I kneel to the flying Goddess whose eye's the whole dusk sky,
birds—robins—talking in the spruce branches, big dry wind, stoned again
to cope with the overload, another class due to suck my wisdom, walking
forked & bewildered in my own naked pronoun . . . in the next dream my
father gestures to me out of the corner phone booth but I can't hear a word
he's saying

JOHN OLIVER SIMON

Robert Rusk

March 30th

[Anna. Steve. Asa]

the average american housewife sneaks 18 times a day

here
be pain
waiting in the nerve
illustrated
by a wave
quanta
he for seconds
relished the word
saw it as
a lot of them
but clearly not
what thought was made of
hopsack
a blackbird would peck it

TOM RAWORTH

well. the film got filmed; looks great, shit, with ann hershey & este gardner on camera, & mary ann harden to do sets—if it flops as a drama, i'll just show it as a silent for the great photography.

angel has been out—& into his own apartment for a month now. we're trying half & half—single every monday, wednesday, & friday; married every tuesday, thursday & saturday, with optional sundays. it's been a relief, i must say—instead of fighting 12 hours a day, we're happy to see each other. *he* got depressed when i insisted on a divorce & since i had spent the evening blaming him (occasionally i fall from sainthood, & simon says blame is my most recurrent sin), he felt the full weight of our recent failures in living together. i told him, actually, "i feel like my body is a traitor. in every other way, i've been able to phase you out of my life." well, harsh words. & he took harsh action. a bottle of dilantin—& by morning, his hearing was temporarily gone. so off to the hospital. jeez, what a winter. both of us trying to do ourselves in. that's what marriage will get you. at any rate, he finally agrees that we are not now good for each other, & must get out, just to survive. but he also says now that the divorce was not all that's wrong for him now; he finally has the job he's been trying to get for 2 years—at a child care center—& he still hates to go to work. he didnt expect that. plus, he's been trying to carry the press load that i've dropped, & it's just too much (which, of course, is why i dropped it). add to that his father's illness & the refusal of all other 7 adult children to take any financial responsibility, & you have one overworked male, with not much going right & a lot going wrong. breakdown.

anyhow, since he's moved out, he's had time to play guitar; i've got my freedom back, so i'm glad to see him when we meet; we go out even on our unmarried nights—went to the a's game Monday; boy, the a's are hot this year. hardly anybody left, & they're whangin the ball all over the park. & friday, he sat next to me at the med, & i'd been talking with all the "office hour" guys, but angel was more interesting than any of them, & there we were again, crazy hot for each other.

ALTA

1

"old lovers are like old apartments,
you wonder how you could've lived there
so long . . ."

Sri Halo Halo

i'm not so sure about april fool's day. this is the time for my
guru, who took a vacation but always comes through when
i'm in need. i don't know about today. i wish you hadn't
assigned it to me. whose idea was this book anyway—and
why are you bothering with the first hundred days of jimmy
carter? i'd rather tell you about the grim grayness of chicago,
or the yellow leaves in paris, or nodding out on the train to
switzerland and thinkin' i was dead, or the trash on the front
steps of my house on haight street. i guess you could say i am
too self-absorbed at this point in my life, but i don't care. did
you know that george sand's statue in the luxembourg
gardens has pigeonshit all over it?

JESSICA HAGEDORN

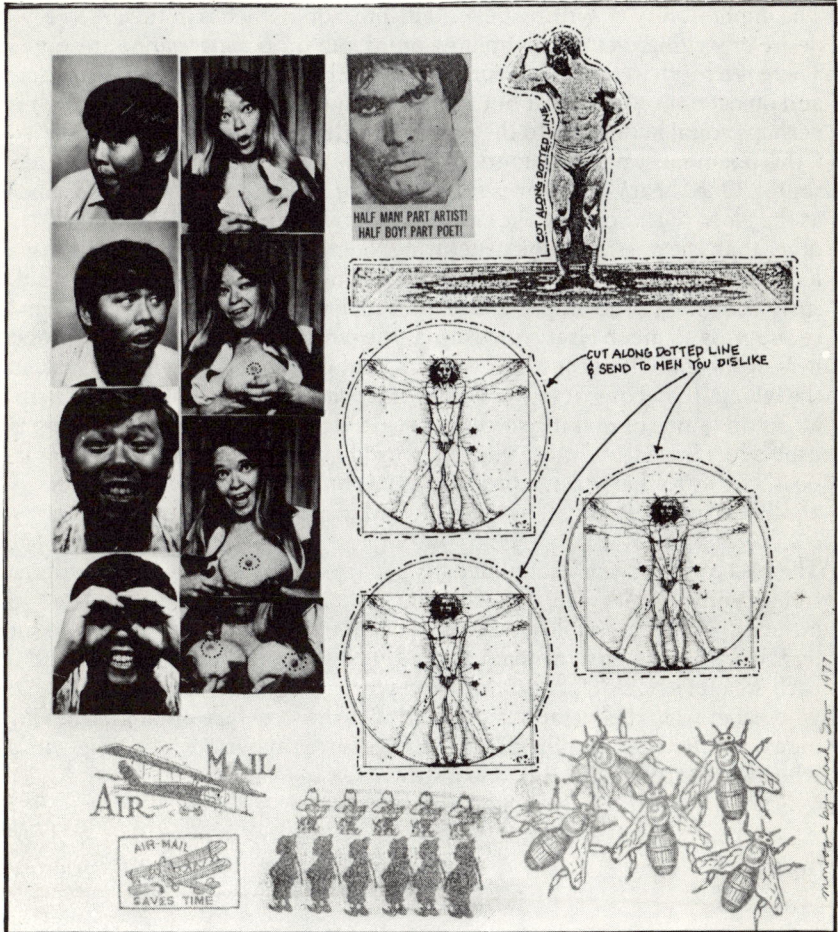

Visions. By a Sexist-Chauvinist Male — a performance play on visual images as perceived in a Capitalist Trained male artist, i.e. the Class Cultural contradictions of Male Art in Capitalism.

JACK LOO

from aRb

The impossibility of writing beyond its horizon, which is in turn the very desire of writing, yet all this spilling of ink out onto paper cannot resolve it. There is a myth in the will to form—that in the well-made phrase, subject and object not only inhabit but are also, somehow, inherent to it, which is perhaps equal in our day to the parallel myth of the legitimacy of voice ("this poem must be read aloud"), as if all this silent scribbling constitutes sound. One "hears" the words of thought alright, but not as noise so much as the *place* of it. Possibly the entire idea of writing, as such, is nothing other than the possibility of structuring the materials of consciousness *into a line*. As if my experience of the world (writing at a kitchen table on an airy spring morning in an empty house) had such form? But to write anything is to suppress so much else: bad writing, the work of incompetents and beginners, is the inability of just this suppression. One wants to tell it all and, in the telling, to become it in some final and primary way. Nothing problematizes this game of making so clearly as does repetition, in which a thing is itself apart from itself: this, this. No word has meaning in the sense that it *possesses* it. Rather, each word has, as its content, all that which is not abolished by it. Negative, as the man said, capability.

The idea of the page is that of negative space, yet it can only occur within a frame, within limits. The opposite (or, more rightly, the opponent) of infinite space. Impossible not to see form in the night sky. A species doomed by the big dipper. In a truly adequate language there would be one word for each idea (event, state, condition) and words would never be repeated. One who believed in the metaphysics could say: the structure of language is an index of fallenness. But the page, the page—we say we are "reading words" when we mean margins, ink and paper.

Ron Silliman

president carter greets secretary of state vance
at the airport upon his return from moscow
as the third world turns
the russians did not have too much to say
they were too busy monitoring the visit
of their president nikoli podgorny to several african nations
they were very interested also in the cuban leader fidel castro
who preceded podgorny before african heads of state
while president carter was busy putting the russians down
over human rights he was also admitting that his welfare reform
would not be ready for quite a while and that his pardon for vietnam
draft evaders would affect only those predominantly white, middle-class
and well educated meanwhile the third world turns
nikoli podgorny makes a surprise visit to somalia
while imelda marcos wins an agreement with col. qaddafi of libya
who has been giving asylum to the moslems of the moro national
liberation front of the philippines during their 5 year war
for independence. the arab moslems will continue oil shipments
to the philippines in exchange for moro independence if king khalid
says its all right. meanwhile fidel castro ends his african tour
hailed as a true human rights liberator for his role in the liberation
struggle of angola and mozambique against the south africans
and rhodesians. on president carter's breakfast table april 3, 1977
james reston has some quotes from state department expert geo kennan
"The question involved in strategic arms talks should not, in my
opinion, have been taken up in isolation. We should have been talking
about wider things . . . and wider political relations too, because
it's all one package," meanwhile imelda marcos visits king khalid of
saudi arabia who is recuperating from an illness in london. he says ok.
meanwhile the heads of state of tanzania, zambia, mozambique, angola
and botswana plan for their meeting on sunday to discuss the visits of
fidel castro and nikoli podgorny. meanwhile president carter and
secretary of state vance read the new york times
as the third world turns.

DAVID HENDERSON

April Fourth

Wake up early: tea, the Chron, and a bowl of muesili. I call up car rental, get car for Nevada; call up Carter's Rental, get shredder for tomorrow. Post Office & off to work. Go to Atlas Saw & get choke flipper & air filter for chainsaw. Up to El Cerrito hills. A breeze. I struggle with chainsaw, it won't adjust, & finally solve the problem. I cut down about 20 small eucalyptus & whack them up in fireplace lengths. About halfway through I see poison oak. The rest of the cutting is done slowly & gingerly until I get too tired. I have one rule: never work with a chainsaw when you're tired. I stop & cool off & think about how much of a discipline it is to work hard & yet avoid wiping your face. I strip off my gloves & smock & think about how ridiculous it must look to wear a smock, yet it's cooler & more lightweight than anything else. Back home I strip & take a soapy shower. Lani fixes me lunch: a chile relleno, noodles & a salad. We discuss money: we don't have any so only cheap chicken from Safeway. I lay down & read about how mummies are made. Around 2 John calls & I go to Nabisco & pick up a load of cardboard for Serendipity. I'm happy to have some cash. I hang around & read magazines & books. According to APR, Marvin Bell's in Tangiers & wondering whether vacations really help a poet produce more poetry; Kenneth Rexroth is attacked as a sexist pig at the age of 72 & he replies, sounding tired of it all. I wonder if anyone's happy with any body else's sexuality. I think about how I negotiated for G.'s tire in Fallon, because he's so obviously queer & ignorant of tires, he might have got charged double. Was I a sexist pig for acquiescing to the dominant social order? (REFRAIN: Back in Old Berkeley again/Back where your thoughts are dead ends). Back to Albany for 2 glasses of white wine & a nap. Then stir-fried rice & black bean sauce chicken. Lani & I do our income tax. I go get a jug of gin with Serendipity's money. Sort out messy letter file & stare at a new poem, entitled VERTIBULLNESS, over a tall glass of gin & tonic. By the time it's gone, I've written this.

KEITH ABBOTT

Somewhere Beyond Plains
April 5, 1977

Hello My Pal,

We had to move. On account of Them.

They come by the house too damn often. Snatched at the chirren. Picked at the dogs. Stole ole bent tin cans, itty bits of grass, a shoe, a shirt, a box of Di-Gel, some plumbing stuff, my hat, one mailbox and a bunch of crushed smokes' packs. *Shoot.* You give 'em an autograph, They want two more. You give 'em two more, They remember a cousin. A Nephew. A Friend. They remember this sad-ass uncle in Moline, living in a home for retired roadmen, who's got a political crush on James Earl. Or Rosey. Lillian. Chip. Amy. Dale.

They got memories. They make demands.

They come at us from everywhere: America, Europe, Spain. They bring cameras and expectations. They spit on shoes. Kick down pickets. They just don't care. They ain't never coming back.

This new house been bothering me. I hear echoes, like in a shell. There's no body of past caught here in the halls and closets and stairwells to cushion the noise of family. It occurs now, and suddenly. This new noise, these feet ringing on formica, how the shower water strikes tiles: it comes to me like applause. Hands, anybody's, any strike of flesh on unsullied equipment, the hollow-ness of places without ghosts. History. Tell you what, pal, you try bein' famous for a while. It blows you up. Then you sputter.

Yours in exile,

Billy Carter

P.S. Jimmy says we'll get used to it. Jody had the same trouble in D.C., but now he's ticking like a clock.

The Jimmy Carter Comic Strip

Last December my band played a Christmas Sales Kickoff Breakfast Meeting for Wards sales managers. I figured it would be like a faculty meeting, all square and full of people who hated what they were doing. Instead the Wards workers were lively and full of wit, even if some of it did suggest that they hated what they were doing. As each supervisor was introduced with a special nickname, the workers roared with laughter. A Chicano sales director was "Taco" Ted Rodriguez, the black furniture man was Bill "Big Boogie" Williams, and, finally, there was a jewelry specialist, Howard "The Happy Okie" Lewis. When the laughter died down he said, "I don't know why I *always* get the Okie business. Hell I'm from Bakersfield!" Bigger laugh. "But it don't bother me anymore, not since we finally elected a President who don't speak funny."

Last night Brother Lee Love, a certified Okie raised near Sacramento, dropped by. He has spent the last six months between the ridiculous and the sublime, a kind of pendulum swinging from LA to Taos and back. Telling him about this writing project, I said I keep hoping I'll write about Carter but I never do. "I want to trust his 'gestures'—Amy in public school and all— but I don't."

Brother Lee was agitated by my comments. In Taos, although busy painting haciendas to earn money, he was taken into a peyote church. They often prayed for Carter. "Everywhere the people are hoping, praying for Carter," he said. "In Taos where everything is thick with potential, even your hands in front of your face, or in LA where it all goes by so fast it's absolutely empty, there is this swelling of people behind Carter."

Brother Lee Love is Brother Lee Love because you believe him. Last night I believed. This morning it's not that I don't believe. It's *so what* the people are hoping and praying for Carter. It's one more display of the benumbed masses on their knees—smoothly enticed there but crawling nevertheless—in fatuous tolerance of the latest Washington political picture. Peel back the picture and the page behind it is still blank, the same old Capitalist zero.

Tom Schmidt

Kalayaan* ay Buang

Kalayaan flops on my belly
in a 4-year-old version of
sky-diving.
                    *Kalayaan ay
buang!* She is crazy
with joy to snuggle with Mom
& me. *Me? Who is this hairy
pink Pollack anyway?*
Will he hit Mom or will he
caress her in the same world
as he does Kalayaan?

"What is this ring?" she queries
in girlie squeek voice
pinching my finger.
"See, it says Vietnam" I reply
"Vietnam people shot down
American bomber plane
& they took metal of the plane
to melt it into a ring
with their name on it."

"Gimme that!" she coyly demands.

"No, Kalayaan. I was on
the island of Cuba & there a comrade
from Vietnam gave me this ring
even as bombs flung down on his people.
As we toasted plum wine I vowed
*'Imperialists will have to cut my
finger off to get this ring'*
that was how deep my feeling ran.
Now I'm giving this ring to your Mom.
Kalayaan, I hope you understand.
Love is solid & hard in revolution.

"The imperialists will have to cut
her finger off to get this ring
yet still I maintain my vow
to the *kasama* from Vietnam.
The finger of the Philippines
will be the same as my own.
Isulong ang Pakikibaka.
As the struggle advances
thru strengths & weakness
thru virtues & failings,
with both our hands
we'll place the stones
of the foundations of the world."

"You silly," she shouts
& smiles a future as broad
as her name,
the Kalayaan of my freedom
as well as her own.

*Kalayaan ay buang means "Freedom is crazy" in Tagalog

HILTON OBENZINGER

Robert Rusk

Love Poem

I shouted in my sleep
'what kind of shoulder
do you have'
'a tanned one' you replied,

you pulled back your blouse
with your lips
the shoulder was pale and lovely.

Still, I reached
the blonde arriving at the volvo
she lifts the silver
sliver of its hand into the sun
the sun is in my eyes
I wake, touching
it, and know your call.

It is that
second thing I wait for.

TOM MANDEL

Scenes Behind the Doors Closed.... A Continuum

I

Marcos and Nixon
cocksuckin' each other
and coming like ballistic
missiles on the spines of the laborers
with Gerald Ford sublimating

II

Marcos and Imelda
feasting on the people's toil
growing fat and looking
more like America every day

III

Gerald Ford eating shit and liking it

IV

President Jimmy Carter claims his "roots" from
a peanut patch
but bordered with a lot of
leafy greens

V

Castro ruling with an iron sugar cane to
satisfy the sweet tooth of the Tiger

VI

Carter lets Castro "play ball"

VII

Nixon plays golf

VIII

Water, water, Everywhere
Then why is it so scarce?
Carter blames it on the lord
while energy companies blame it
on the bosa nova

IX

Carter and Andrew Young do a soft shoe shuffle
for the United Nations to the tune of
Knock, knock, knocking on S. Africa's door

X

Carter completes his 101 days in office
using the same card tricks dealt
behind the flag

Drawing by Demerie Faitler for Jack Loo

from The Scheme of Things
(from 2197)

Language in which sensitivity information. The lower the this, the higher
the noise. These are only handguns and have no other sex. This locating is
not the concept of the difficulty there was. End events are development
here. Take of this, read of that. Forms from the insect fill. Blind, we decide,
is color talking. High tide of rain forms in the low fog. Feeding the woman,
kill the popcorn. Searches of the world. A song I mylar kite to warrior.
Proliferation of the alphabet.

Forearm of volleyball and day without swollen. World swollen from a full
day of pomegranates. Coming to the form of rain with the greatest loss.
Objective distance becomes in object. Body as older, as loss of shapeless-
ness. The truth is full of power. Pastel concentric to circles. Block of gas
thought, water, small hum in the lightbulb as I make my carving. Grains
nuts bowl. If the sound becomes water, gas jets becomes hum. As he made
matches, his wax drifted into Mexico. The recognition of my greatest self.
Poems should not have goals.

Loss of vision, loss of weight. This language brings in the summer choices of
the genuine. Window was more open than the room. A new distance of
roaches had meaning in our verification. Do what I made. Each one pulls
his page on, one chosen at a random. The sleepers bus a way that readily
work. The village arrived with fishing first. This in an envelope of meaning.
We went loomy by sailing, air by through. The definition of certain. Inserts
or the art of posited from the flight of random. Sea sprinkled the kelp of my
former popcorn.

RON SILLIMAN

how seductive that flow is sitting here in the streetcar now and not wanting
to write looking out the window not wanting any language but what goes
by in a stream babbling not to stop it in any way still it it pours through the
window same as the sun constant I could go to sleep in it

Arguing, arguing, I was arguing with myself earlier this morning that all
experience is verbal, that everything has to be mediated by language finally
or we just don't know where we are. Language is the matrix, the *prima
materia*, this mother's body. The ooze and blood. Mud. Billboards. Dirty
language. Or: (Pound) "Rhythm is a form cut into TIME. . . ." Dirty time,
dirty mother, we plink, plink, plinked your heart out, for a road sign, for a
song.

Language isn't free. There is a price. "The death of a thousand cuts." Coal.
Oil. Water, It runs out. "Liar, liar, pants on fire."

10:45 p.m.: My last day and I feel like I've evaded the assignment—don't I
ever think about Jimmy Carter? But I was thinking plenty about him and his
cohorts yesterday afternoon reading the breakdown on the proposals they
presented at the last SALT meeting. It turns out that "arms reduction"
means they'll actually wind up with more nuclear warheads than they have
now if they get what they're bargaining for. That's what "arms reduction"
means. And I thought for a long time about the word: "warhead."

"Warhead" is a fairly surreal word.

I had the sense of the language going up in smoke around us.

> "No chance for me to live, Mother,
> You might as well mourn."

BEVERLY DAHLEN

I'm horrified to discover how competitive I am. Is everybody? Here's T—, my good and dear friend, I love her poems, think they are massive and deep and despairing and jaunty with great language, and we're in the workshop together. But today, both of us reading in Mark's "Writers on Writing" class, I'm thinking "She's too good, will they think I'm nothing in comparison, will they like my reading as much, and besides she's young and sexy how can an old lady like me compete even just reading poems?"

And then I'm ashamed to be thinking such a thing and I rejoice in how terrific her poems are. But I'm still not happy because I want to be "best". Today is my day to send my journal to Steve. Will I send this??

Contrast at the reading—between our two insect poems. Her "Fly" poem is an identification. In the end she accepts the insect into her world. My "Drought" poem is the reverse. I hate the wasps and really try to come to terms with my hatred. In my series of "cancer" poems it's clear that I'm not sure who's the patient and who's the disease, so it seems necessary for me to identify the villain. In the immune system, white cells cure (the patient) and kill (the cancer cells), so I'd damn well better know which is which. In the poem the wasps are the enemy and I'd better be sure of it. But to recognize the enemy—is not necessarily to know it as evil, particularly when it's yourself.

Her poem, though it seems "healthier", wouldn't do for me right now. But two days after I wrote mine, when more wasps invaded my cabin, I was miserable watching them die in the insect spray. Ecology. Vegetarianism. Sentimentality. We eat. What we eat we kill. I wish I could better understand the relationship of T's loving poem to my hating one. Poetry. New connections. Identify. Or kill? Eat? Stay alive?

I've always been so sure that one should never kill (or fight) in cold blood . . .

Frances Jaffer

serafino malay syquia
pilipino poet

i did not know

you would keep
the silence

tied down
thick
in banana leaves

i saw you
bending

folding

like kugon grass
hugging the snow

tomorrow

you will have visions

wallowing
in a fresh field
of wild carabaos

and your voice

will be heard
loud and clear
as the igorote wind

kapatid tagatac
did not know
you ran off
in a winter loin cloth

AL ROBLES

15

Carter Drops His Plan for $50 Tax Rebate

JACK FROST

Tin-Tan* cooks. Spills high energy onto
Valencia St. Old winitos wander in our door looking for memories of good times & old friends and
find instead, a neat machine drilled with words,
images and color.

This road been traveled on for years now and
still many bridges to cross—but I can feel the light
of this Saturday and can feel the strength that we
make of this afternoon/ the future of our labor/
the satisfaction of giving it out all/ coming in to
port from a stormy sea.

Our vision is wide angle. Collective labor
from collective dreams.

*Tin-Tan, a tabloid of poems, stories and articles published in the Mission District of San Francisco.

ALEJANDRO MARQUIA

April 17 Cluster

I had a friend who was sick and he sat for two days at a
bus stop unable to move.
Later he said that it had seemed like only a minute or
two and that during all that time he thought he saw a
single red and silver bus half a block away and approaching;
he was only waiting for it to arrive and then he would
stand up.
Now it is Sunday and it used to be that nobody worked
except preachers

while these objects are swollen by my interest in them
a light and in a light the luster

not murder and clover
an inspiration to heroes and danger
is a grief or anger sadness
worry is harmful from here
the children and honesty the very air
and water we drink

necessity is invisible but it sticks
now I've returned to the countryside
and now hidden I am gone
while it lies on the ground
where the fence poles are notched by the hens
and fits where it sits in the sky
out of the window the wasps have returned
and bees to the collards are gone to flower
and likewise the broccoli
and the daffodils are dry
instead the reals

heroes

horrors

help and health

hark and heap

LYN HEJINIAN

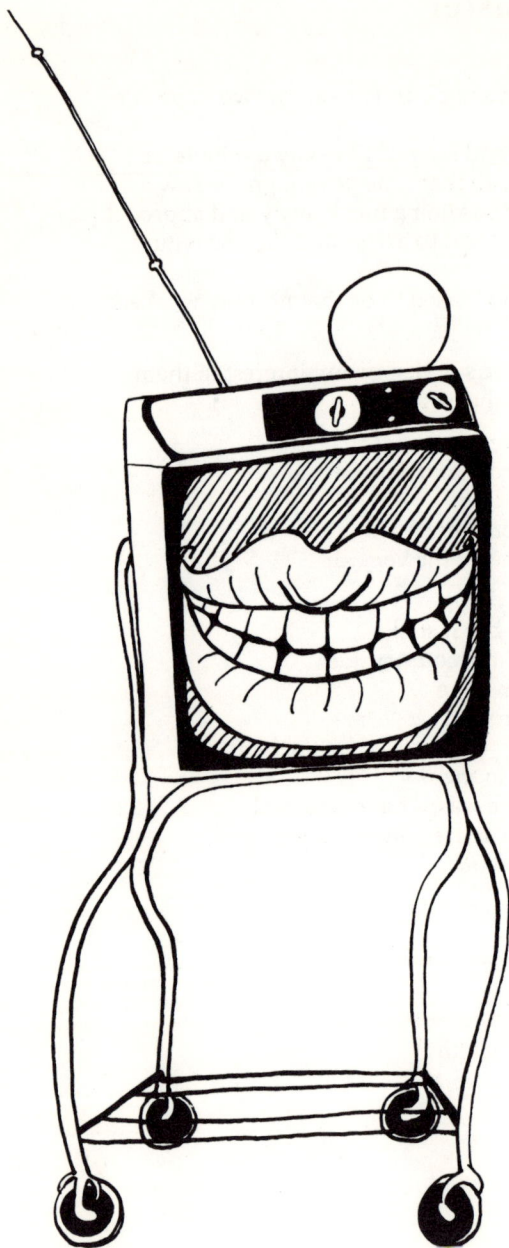

DEBRA McGEE

i'm the mother of a teenager. simon is freaking out about turning 35. this year has been rough on me that way; especially after angel said he wanted someone "younger & prettier." who needs that? not some lady turning 35, i can tell you. what makes me really mad is that 34 is sposed to be the hottest year sexually for a woman, & i spent the whole damn year worrying whether angel was the final word; & how much love has to do with sex, & what the hell i'm supposed to do to get laid with a lot of thrills & a lot of love. at least i had a few good ones; i mean, it wasnt a total desert; but it sure wasnt the hot time i'd been promised in the books, & i blame that remark for inhibiting me so much with angel that i cant even get on top, or be naked with the lights on. jeez. what a frost. it's a wonder i can even get off.

ah, i'm supposed to be writing about carter. another state stomps in the e.r.a. great. "the trouble with democracy is that it's so damn slow," said art goldberg last nite. god, for real. where else do women have to beg just to get equal job treatment? i used to feel all happy that i lived here, where i could create my own press. if we had the e.r.a., i might not NEED a separate press.

as far as how it is for women now, i think it's the shits. more prostitution than there's been for years, constant violence against women in the media; i wish i could do with my life what is possible for a human to do, & stop wasting my time with the artie mitchells of the world. what we could be, jesus. healers, visionaries; loving people tuning into the whole cosmos. instead, we have to have these dorquey meetings every saturday to see which theater we're going to picket next. instead of yoga i have to learn kung fu. what can i say? fix it, carter? the attitude that he can fix it & i cant is the most dangerous of all. so i cant even say that.

i look forward to the day when all people refuse to mistreat all other people. & i'm glad i have people to love, who love me.

Beyond Plains
April 19, 1977

Hello My Pal,

Here is how it all happened, step by step.
1. The Agent put me on the Tour   2. The Tour is continual
3. I go places and speak   4. For money   5. I speak clearly
6. About what's on my mind   7. Or nothing   8. Tell jokes
9. Same old jokes   10. Like in politics   11. Everybody listens
12. But in Nashville   13. It got bad   14. The Jaycees pay well
15. But serve up rancid chicken   16. I got to feeling poorly
17. The Agent sent me to another place   18. Who knows where
19. With tables and chickens   20. Somebody tapped a water glass
21. I spoke   22. The faces in front   23. Were round and red as
mine   24. I forgot who I was   25. I became what I was in that
moment   26. Or became the sum of what   27. Was coming back
at me   28. The reflection   29. Or image   30. It was confusing
31. But gave me distance   32. Distance is eyes   33. The eyes have
it.   34. I seemed to see   35. Clear to the District   36. Where one
hand   37. Was washing another   38. Same two hands   39. As
ever   40. I saw Jimmy and waved   41. But he turned from me
42. Like he was embarrassed   43. Around him were men   44. In
dark suits   45. Suits dark as broken promises   46. Or fresh
blood   47. From a dark source   48. They were taking him
49. Into a building   50. Same building   51. As ever   52. The
sound of machines   53. Like threshers   54. Filled my head   55. I
wanted to tell him   56. My brother   57. Before he
disappeared   58. That no thing   59. Was more real than any other
60. That all things   61. Were equally possible   62. In this world
63. Which is the story told   64. At empty tables   65. But it was
66. Too late   67. I could taste dollars   68. On my tongue
69. And the sound of machines and broken stones   70. And felled
trees   71. And dammed rivers   72. Got louder and louder
73. Until I sank into the suck of it   74. And vanished amid
75. The familiar depradations.

So long for now,

Billy Carter

the pervasiveness of language
as if we lived in it
down there
This beginning, for instance, *in medias res,* in which we find ourselves looking at
any thing
which is invisible
not because it is not there but because it is everywhere constantly
(a tree   a rock)
and so it seems to be
a given.

Its otherness is awesome. It is that grace which we praise
and can in no way alter.

Which
nevertheless
in time
we alter.

We walk in the city, the 5 o'clock sun slanting against the crowds.

Everywhere
looking into that face
which we do not recognize
in which we cannot
find ourselves

how shall we say it, claim it? its substance
broken into the bricks and tar
of Market Street.
"My love"   I should say
and would you turn
and know me

everything blares
shuffles in silence

Therefore this language, this *prima materia*
against which I lay my hand
these lines
these turnings
as if it were my life.

Beverly Dahlen

My 35th birthday/ tripping on acid/ with Jan/ on the hawk hill in
Strawberry Canyon/ furl of poison oak smoke rising from a Control
Burn miles downcanyon headed our way/ above the sharp yellow/ layer
of poison air/ day after Carter's energy message/ which I didn't hear

vulnerability of our space here/ shrinking revenues/ biocrystals/
protect this nervous/ trembling flesh/ for a moment/ no refuge from
glare of/ "for better or worse"/ someone's teeth among the poppies

I nuzzle my chin into a fork of stone/ I feel my father's shape of
skull inside mine/ unable to tell the difference between blue & green
to his deathbed/ Jan's turquoise/ blue Krishna fucking/ faded blue
jeans/ wore green hat/ debris of lupine/ pattern of these waving hills

no way to breathe here, pack out of mucksmoke over chapparal peak/
bluejay irritably scribbling/ tell the truth the whole truth & nothing
but the truth yr honor/ help ye god/ I am caught in the web/ caught
irretrievably in seeing it/ and caught by choice in saying it/ just
when I see the whole web almost perfect/ have to break to say it/ and
as I struggle in saying I see more & more/ no limit

couldn't breathe there either/ trail down northside tup-tupping on
recorder like an unskilled taoist/ finally achieved clarity/ by the
little railroad where it cuts thru a bluff/ slanting brick-crimson
bake-layer of pliocene lava/ a rockpile with lizards & paintbrush,
further down, mule's ears

I said Happy Birthday/ to everything/ yerba buena leaf-lips, black
ant on rockpattern/ last year's live oak/ kneeling/ Happy Birthday/
because it is the same age I am/ stuck my hand into what/ mammalian
secretion/ my own pee/ back to everything/ Happy Birthday/ to you too
suckers in your/ airplane crossing the sun

2 lizards courtship dance a slow hour/ female languid, tail erect,
scuttles a few inches/ male follows hot to trot doing frantic pushups
displaying lust/ they fuck indistinct among leaves & afterwards lie
wasted on separate rocks

Jan all day for me a rock/ a flower, paintbrush/ sweet smell of bread
& coconut oil/ grin solid understanding/ my wife/ we've given rings &
vows/ she gave me the moon, space-time & beyond & everyman & some
underwear/ I wanted the great american poem for my birthday too/
she looked everywhere, on the avenue/ but nobody had one

JOHN OLIVER SIMON

Yerington, Nevada,
City Center Motel, RM 11.

I wake up about 5:30, make some black tea with my handydandy
water coil and sit down in front of my typewriter. My hero is in
Arkansas, driving to Tulsa with catatonic Glenice in the back seat
whimpering. Poor Percy. I write all about how lonely he is and
how sorry he is about handing Glenice over to her mother without
ever explaining how she got so crazy. I finish and wonder what's
next. I haven't the faintest. I outline new characters & their epi-
sodes. Hello Jaundice Cahn: I can't wait to get to you. I walk out
to Main St. and check the jeweler's shop for the time. Someday I'll
buy a watch. I check to see if all the kids' poetry is typed up, then
off to high school. I don't want to work today so I have them do
cutups. Those goosey 10th grade girls come up with the best line of
the day: *"What women should know about impotence in males is
to think big."* Thank you Readers Digest, if I had to rely on text-
books for cutups nothing would be even remotely interesting. I
split, throw everything in the car, check out and buy 2 beers.
About 5 miles out of town, I pull over and open a Coors and light
up a joint. 3 hits & I'm off. Suddenly the desert is very interesting.
I chuckle about how interesting it is. About halfway to Carson
City I see a sign saying Virginia City. I pull a screeching U-ie &
head up in the hills. I stop in at Silver City hippie bar. Whiskey. I
see Denise & Coleen. Hi. Denise tells me about some of the intrica-
cies she's spotted in GUSH. I toast her for it, Happy Trip to
Alaska. I drive through Virginia City & an old student pulls me
over. We talk. Then I start down toward Reno. Some Chevy's
close behind me, I decide to race him. 50 mph, taking the curves
terrific. About halfway down I realize I'm totally smashed &
should stop all this nonsense. I drive slow until I pull into Lorelle's
driveway. She's not home. I dump my stuff & lay down and listen
to my heart calm down. Driving revs me up. I drink whiskey. Get
crazy. Go outside & sit on a stump & blank out enough to feel the
wind go through my body. Remember clearly how I used to sit in
the Northwest woods and do that day after day as a kid. I fall
asleep on Lorelle's bed. Wake up, it's dusk. I decide to go into
Reno and see FUN WITH DICK & JANE. Rrrmmmmm, down-

town. Ain't on no more, so backout to massive gigantic biggie all fun movie center 4 SHOWS center and see THE LATE SHOW. Odd movie. Some time I shall analyze thoroughly what's wrong. Maybe when I get back in Berkeley with my intellectual friends. Back out to Lorelle's. She's in bed asleep. I tiptoe in & pour whiskey for dinner. It's my weekend, isn't it? Besides, I had popcorn. Lorelle wakes in mild panic. It's me. We talk, or rather I talk & she rambles in her sleep. Last day at Art Commission, she's through, but sick. Big day tomorrow: free steaks & company. I sit & look at the pine woods as she falls asleep. Drink more whiskey. Try to decide if I've eaten anything all day but popcorn. More whiskey. Slowly I come back to myself. Hello Keith. I take that Keith & put him to bed. Tomorrow he'll be the only one to wake up. That other guy'll be gone.

KEITH ABBOTT

There is an Incessant Party Goin' On Downstairs...

There is an incessant party goin' on downstairs/ there's a band that's moved in next door. R & B music blaring at eight o'clock in the morning/ like waking up in your car in the middle of a nightmare and realizing you been cruising down MacArthur Blvd. all the while/ Thelma Houston chanting don't/ leave me/ this wayyyyy...'

It's rude/ it's annoying/ you get a headache with that incessant party goin' on downstairs. It makes you long for valiums and coffee and cocaine all at once/ just to get you straight by nine o'clock/ which is an ungodly hour anyway/ so you can figure out who the fuck is dancing to all this loud music/ so early in the day/

It's been goin' on since dawn, i'm sure/ i mean my cells are not ready for sleazing when the sun is out/ parties and sleazing have certain rules about them/ the sun is not quite the proper thing to have around/ if you know what i MEAN/ the sun is a little too harsh and healthy/ sequins always seem a little loud at ten in the morning/ cosmetics a mere circus/

There is no ambience in the daytime/ the daytime and the almighty sun are for kids/ grannies/ bizness/ banks/ church/ and runny grits and eggs/ it's the time to be asleep curled up against your lover's crotch like a spoon/ not time for this incessant, driving, full orchestra that explodes up through my wooden floor/ makin' me EVIL/

makin' me wanna push pins through my Erica Jong doll/ upstage Richard Pryor/ comb Patti Smith's hair/ keep goin' like i been goin'/ ignoring news-papers/ television/ voter registration/ the IRS/ the ERA/ Jimmy Carter/ Amy Carter/ and the entire brood that lives in a place that has nothing to do with me/ with this incessant party goin' on downstairs in my life/ with the trash on the front steps of my house/ with the young junkies loitering one block away/ hundreds of them/ asleep in the deep/ young/ and some-times/ still/ so beautiful

JESSICA HAGEDORN

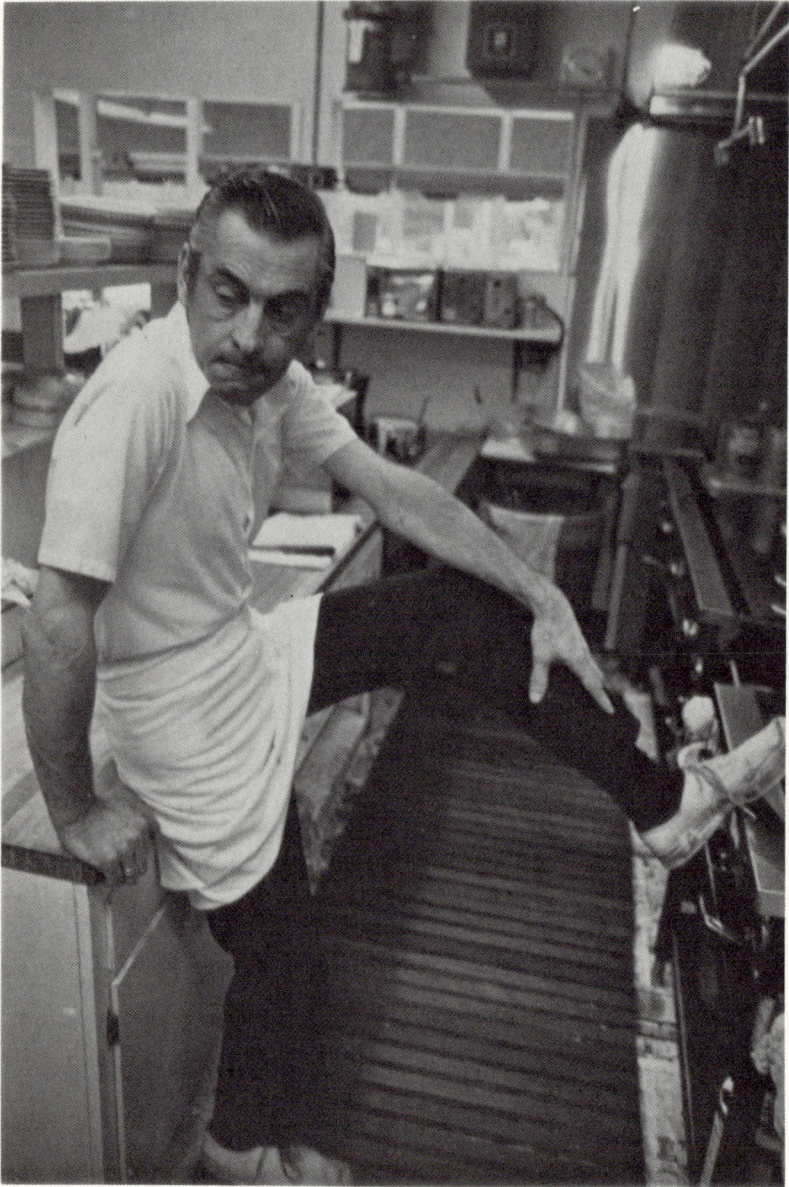

ROBERT RUSK

The American River II

At night the American River is unbelievably still. From the old bridge I see the water has a skin of soft glass, and it is waiting—to reflect the moon some other night, to move the fish that are asleep in its belly. The cars crossing the Sunrise Bridge downstream are noisy and their lights shoot thin red and yellow flames upriver. In the daytime it is difficult to be aware of the cars, they seem miniature and distant, so it's as if the nighttime pushes the light and noise down onto the river where they splash violently. In the same way the houses along the bluff are nearly invisible behind trees during the day. At night they crowd along the edge, rudely lighted and ostentatious.

Previous nights I have seen great owls and (nearer to dusk) tiny bats fly swiftly among the girders of the bridge. I have run into people fighting, smoking dope, drinking tequila, making love, telling big lies, and once, on a very dark summer evening, a boy walked up to me as I stood watching the river and asked me if I wanted to buy a gun, this .38. I could see his silhouette, the small clouds of his white t-shirt and shaggy blonde hair, and between us the weak glitter of the chrome-plated revolver. I said no, and he went away. Tonight the bridge is deserted. There is a slight breeze, and I can feel the bridge vibrate faintly each time it comes up. The vibration is a distant hum in the steel, like a fading tuning fork. A single owl screams very close to me, but I see nothing. There is a small but perfectly clear splash under the bridge.

As I walk home the town is quiet and most of the lights are out. It is much later than I thought, and I must have been standing on the bridge for a long time, waiting.

TOM SCHMIDT

International Hotel:
A Way of Living
Followed by Many Men

"General William Tecumseh Sherman was living somewhere
in 'rooms' and dining at the International
occasionally with his friend, Captain Folsom, who had been
a classmate at West Point—a way of living
followed by many men, so that the table d'hote was
quite a center of the City's life . . ."

Wahat hangs out the window at the crowd:
"You are my bread and water. You my support. We poor. Dis
is our home. So many Pilipinos not allowed to live anybear else
dat's why we stay here. We were not allowed to have
home any place in city. Discrimination so much.
We need low-cost housing. Tank you!"

In the basement that was once the "Hungry I" club Lenny Bruce
makes ironic snickers at the Mayor
& beatnik disgust of the 50's whips away
into the torn-down Bataan pool hall & manila Cafe
"Remember me, Mr. Banducci? I was your busboy. This is my home."

"The International is first-class in all its appointments.
There are 142 rooms for guests with many conveniently arranged
suites for families whose comfort and convenience is a subject
of special attention by the proprietor."

Just old men. Where else could they cross the street
to buy pancit & fish? The law said they could
not marry. Now they are old. "We are drawn together.
come from the same place. We feel at home here." We are
at the heart of love
because so many come to defend them.

"Governor Johnson has just sent for me. He is at the
International Hotel on Jackson St. My belief is that the
leaders of the vigilantes are not able to control their
men, and that they will be forced to extremity . . ."

The demonstration wraps around the building like a disciplined
        bear hug.
                        The Sheriff is scared.
The Transamerica Pyramid looms over like one
        of Dracula's teeth. Nude encounter parlors delve
deep into pockets of the foolish. Yet old men
won't be traded in for parking-lots.
All of their hopes bob up and down in the crowd
like white-caps in a big oil-slick.

"*They were to be kept moving, remain transit. They stayed in
rooming houses, hotels and labor camps. The International Hotel
was one of these. 'Manilatown' became a permanent settlement,
a convenient culture contact. It was the dispatch point for
jobs in the Alaska fishing industry. It was the home workers
returned to, where merchant marines lived while in port, where
distant relatives and friends could be contacted. It was a
way of living followed by many men.*"

Somebody decided what was America.
Somebody discovered gold.
Quickly, someone
stole a state & decided it was united.
They came to the Hotel, to the hub of gold,
& they argued
The pro-slave state Supreme Court Justice
& the anti-slave US Senator from the new-stolen
State of Califas circa 1854.
They take ten steps & shoot it out.
Somebody decided who was America.
The landlord decided.
the Pinoys, they are no deposit no return.
Somebody else decided.
Somebody else decided wrong.
The Pinoys, they will decide where to live,
they built this place,
it's theirs & at a price they can afford.
It's simple.
The crowd circles the Hotel, hub of a great wheel.
We decide. We are the heart of history.

HILTON OBENZINGER

—my last entry in the "Jimmy Carter Day Book" and I need to write about the process. Anything so self-conscious that aspires to being a real "journal" is not likely to succeed—at least, not in being a "real journal". What it *can* be is mysterious; we will probably only know when everybody's entries are in and in place. If this were my real journal, today, I would be writing extremely personal things about my life: about my son who just left (he lives out of town) after spending a long week-end with us; about some of my physical symptoms which are a nuisance; and about the anxiety I am experiencing for some unknown reason (except of course that it must have to do with my son's visit and departure). But that is all too personal for public exposure.

I can't tell from the last "Day Book"* how this problem worked out—perhaps we cannot be sure. What seemed open and unself-conscious I now realize was probably not. Even if, as one participant says he is doing, we wrote our journals every day and were assigned our dates afterwards, I think I'd simply have 100 days of public document instead of private journal.

And the fact that the days are chosen in advance, arbitrarily, further distorts the process. You (who are you?) might assume from my past entries that I never think about politics. In fact that's not true; it just happened that on my assigned days I was thinking about something else. A complete journal would be full of anger and frustration about Carter's politics, about abortion law revisions, etc. I spend hours on political considerations, magazines, T.V. news programs, telephone conversations, letters and telegrams to legislators, participation in feminist activities wherever they relate to women's literature. And my head is full of Nuclear Proliferation, African civil wars and American and Russian intervention, drought relief, and such problems.

As for Carter, I didn't hope for much, but I thought at least he might be a feminist. When I saw Costanza and Califano I lost even that hope. It's pretty sad and pretty scary; I don't feel there's much an individual citizen can do. One system as well as another degenerates to power plays and people being restrained or suffering— a reformer dies and his system is corrupted by the people who get control.

So I continue to put my efforts into grass roots feminist aesthetic movements, where I think some real changes may be occurring. Because I'm convinced that nothing short of root psychological changes in human psychology can do much to improve life on Earth.

FRANCIS JAFFER

*"The Day Book, February 1 thru April 1, 1974" Shocks Magazine #5, published by Momo's Press February 1975. It included six writers: Andrei Codrescu, Beverly Dahlen, Susan Griffin, Jessica Hagedorn, Roberto Vargas and Stephen Vincent.

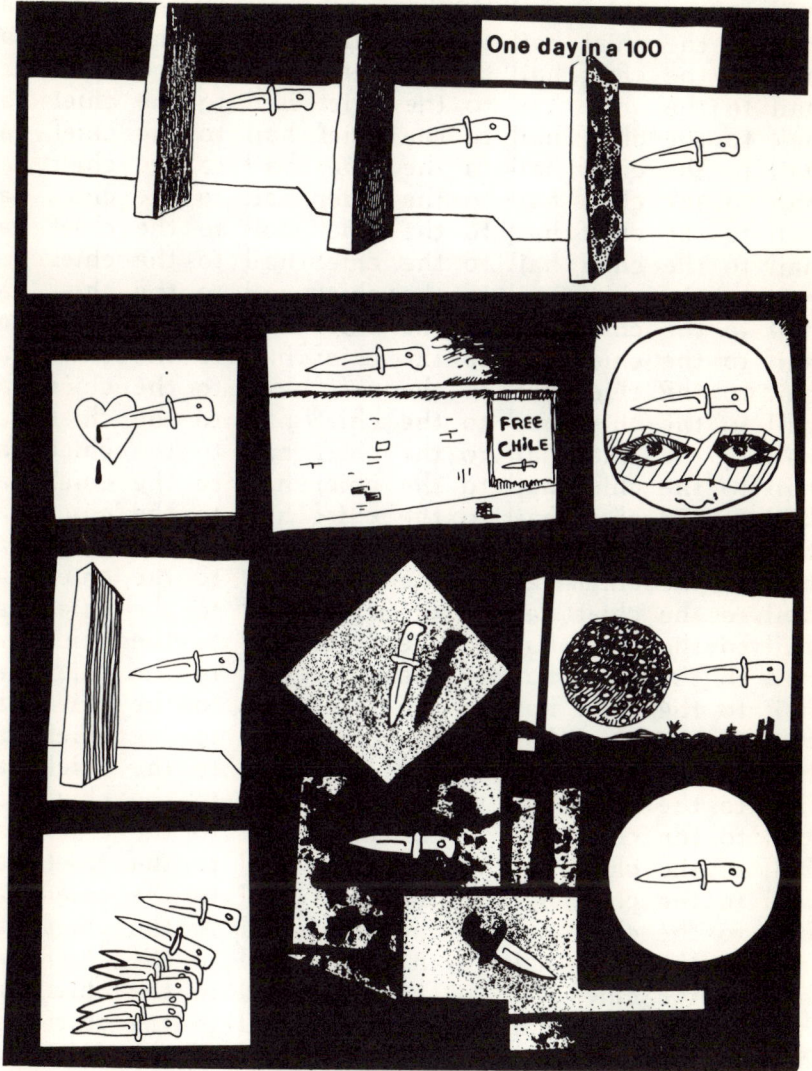

RENE YANES

hail to the chief hail to the chief hail to the chief hail
hail to the chief hail to the chief hail to the chief hail
hail to the chief hail to the chief hail to the chief hail
hail to the chief hail to the chief hail to the chief hail
hail to the chief hail to the chief hail to the chief hail
hail to the chief hail to the chief hail to the chief hail
hail to the chief hail to the chief hail to the chief hail
hail to the chief hail to the chief hail to the chief hail
hail to the chief hail to the chief hail to the chief hail
hail to the chief hail to the chief hail to the chief hail
hail to the chief hail to the chief hail to the chief hail
hail to the chief hail to the chief hail to the chief hail
hail to the chief hail to the chief hail to the chief hail
hail to the chief hail to the chief hail to the chief hail
hail to the chief hail to the chief hail to the chief hail
hail to the chief hail to the chief hail to the chief hail
hail to the chief hail to the chief hail to the chief hail
hail to the chief hail to the chief hail to the chief hail
hail to the chief hail to the chief hail to the chief hail
hail to the chief hail to the chief hail to the chief hail
hail to the chief hail to the chief hail to the chief hail
hail to the chief hail to the chief hail to the chief hail
hail to the chief hail to the chief hail to the chief hail
hail to the chief hail to the chief hail to the chief hail
hail to the chief hail to the chief hail to the chief hail
hail to the chief hail to the chief hail to the chief hail
hail to the chief hail to the chief hail to the chief hail
hail to the chief hail to the chief hail to the chief hail
hail to the chief hail to the chief hail to the chief hail
hail to the chief hail to the chief hail to the chief hail
hail to the chief hail to the chief hail to the chief hail
hail to the chief hail to the chief hail to the chief hail
hail to the chief hail to the chief hail to the chief hail
hail to the chief hail to the chief hail to the chief hail
hail to the chief hail to the chief hail to the chief hail
hail to the chief hail to the chief hail to the chief hail
hail to the chief hail to the chief hail to the chief hail
hail to the chief hail to the chief hail to the chief hail
hail to the chief hail to the chief hail to the chief hail
hail to the chief hail to the chief hail to the chief hail

DAVID HENDERSON

His first
100 days

JACK FROST

Objects are alienated by labor.

Musicians moved me all night.

She took my ankles.
It was a beautiful storm.
I moved upstairs & downstairs.
I was not a quiet man.
There was a new regime.
I lost touch with Carter.
He was in a small room
figuring it out.

"Lysol cleans baths without water." (KSFX advertisement)

"Use a glass of water to brush your teeth
and you will save 10 gallons of water." (KSFX drought solver)

Does it / Did it take 10 gallons?

Zaire is a vision:
      Russian Bombers Sweep Near Our Border (Examiner Headline)
      Water Please Water Please
Women will unionize. The grief grows less
in the heart. Will the Baptist give us
a soft spot for change. Is work
the alternative to consumption. When
I work do I consume less or more.
Does unemployment create less
or more. Who is What
consuming. Stay calm. If
I put a hand on Debra's belly
I feel a heel or a back or a
hand. Carter puts a blind fold
on, puts his hand around the
globe and says it's great to
know you're pregnant. Is this
hot spot Zaire or the Chinese/
Soviet border? This cool spot -
is it the channel between Georgia
& Cuba? How can I tell Nebraska
from the Ukraine?

The residual grief of a history of.

I wish language could be complex,
subtle and popular. Eat your cake
Shakespeare.

Ice crackers were seen taking chips
in the park. I desire warm
trees.

Carter says how can I be born if I'm
on top. Let's exchange summits
everybody. You're already out of it
South Africa.

STEPHEN VINCENT

The
PENNSYLVANIA
St. Petersburg
Florida

April 29th

TOM RAWORTH

MICHAEL MYERS